Return on Marketing Investment

Return on Marketing Investment

Demand More from your Marketing and Sales Investments

Guy R. Powell

Albuquerque ◆ Atlanta ◆ Boca Raton

ISBN: 0-9718598-1-7

Library of Congress Control Number: 2003090524

Printed in the United States of America
10 9 8 7 6 5 4 3

Although the author has made every effort to ensure the accuracy and completeness of information contained in this book, we assume no responsibility for errors, inaccuracies, omissions, or any inconsistency herein. Any slights of people, places, or organizations are unintentional.

First Printing 2002.

Attention Corporations, Universities, Colleges, and Professional Organizations: Quantity discounts are available on bulk purchases of this book for educational purposes. Special books or book excerpts can also be created to fit specific needs. For information, please visit www.returnonmarketing.net.

Dedication

To my wife, Karen, for putting up with me.

To my son, Robert.

To Collin and Kristin.

To the many great sales and marketing individuals, customers and partners that I have had the pleasure to work with and learn from.

To the children of the United Methodist Children's Home. The mission of The United Methodist Children's Home is to serve the needs of children and their families in crisis. Ten percent of the profits derived from the sale of this book will be contributed to this worthy charity. If you would like to learn more about the United Methodist Children's Home, please contact them directly at 500 S. Columbia Drive, Decatur, GA 30030, or www.umch.com.

Table of Contents

Index

Bibliography

Acknowledgements

Thanks to the many people who have made this book possible, either with direct input and feedback or with input throughout my marketing career:

Mark Browning, Former VP Marketing, eDeltacom
Teresa Caro, Director, Marketing, KnowledgeStorm, Inc.
Rich Grady, Managing Director, VIA NET.WORKS USA
Bernd Harzog, President & CEO, KevSoft, Inc.
Joan Herbig, President & CEO, XcelleNet, Inc.
Jack Koch, Former VP Marketing, 3Com
Bob Kornecki, Global Practice Leader, Edelman Public
  Relations Worldwide
Dr. Fritz Kroeger, Former Partner, ATKearney
Brad Lindeman, President, Matrix Controls, Inc.
Bill Marks, Vice President Public Relations, Coca-Cola North
  America
Dave Owen, President & CEO, ImageServe
Robert F. Pierry, Jr., President, Roger Bullivant of Texas, Inc.
Lloyd Powell, President, Richmond Products, Inc.
Wendy Stroud, President, Stroud & Associates, Ltd.
Moira Vetter, President, Cracker Communications, Inc.

Thanks to Beth Powell for helping me wade through the commas, the numbers and providing invaluable feedback on content and consistency in thought. I couldn't have done it without her.

Many thanks to Larry Warnick and Chris Adelman, Founding Partners of Coacta Business Group, for acting as a great sounding board as I wrote this book. They provided invaluable input and feedback as I worked through many of the Return on Marketing Investment concepts.

A special thanks to James Cogswell, President, Cogswell Asset Management, and fellow University of Chicago Graduate School of Business MBA alumnus, who provided me with valuable feedback on a wide range of issues.

Preface

When I first began writing this book I thought it would be completed within a few months. Well, it has now been over a year and it has finally been declared done, although I am sure there will be another version or two that will need to be written. With every day of experience and interaction with other marketing and business professionals, I learn something that could easily be added.

Over the past 20 years or so, I have worked with many highly-successful sales, marketing and business professionals, and I have learned something from every one of them. This book contains the compilation of those experiences synthesized into a systematic marketing planning and management process. In order to illustrate many of these points, I have developed a number of examples. Many of these examples have been developed in order to illustrate the particular point as clearly as possible. In most cases, they don't represent the more complex business situation, which simply can't be accurately reproduced in this writing. In addition, any numbers presented typically do not represent actual situations, but have been changed so as not to reveal any confidential information for these companies.

Marketing programs at the lowest level are defined as simply a direct mail piece, a newsletter campaign or an advertising campaign. At a higher level, these programs can be defined as a complete overhaul in the channel strategy or product development plan. At the highest level, it has to do with developing a strategy for the company to meet and exceed the goals of the investors. Each of these is executed with the goal of gaining the highest revenue for a given level of investment.

With that in mind, there are two main points that I believe set this book apart:

- Investments in marketing must provide a significantly higher return than investing in the sales team; otherwise, why not take the same money and allocate it to hire more salespeople?
- Investments in marketing (and for that matter, any investment made by a business) must provide a higher return for higher risk, less certain programs.

It also seems that marketing has often not sold itself very well, neither internally nor externally. Many business folks think that marketing is all about colors, graphics and creative slogans. This couldn't be further from the truth. In the end, for any business, the most successful marketing folks know that it is all about sales and generating leads that lead to sales. Marketing is an integral component of the revenue generating process. It is just selling at another level.

Certainly, colors, graphics and slogans are important, and from a consumer marketing perspective, these aspects of marketing can make an enormous difference. With consumer marketing and potentially even some business-to-business marketing, simply the level of creativity in a particular campaign can impact sales, usually in a very positive way. With business-to-business marketing, it is more the unglamorous bump-and-grind of fighting for every nickel of revenue possible.

Colors, graphics and good design are also important for effective business-to-business marketing. These right-brain activities must still be done properly. However, the emphasis needs to be more on content, value proposition, differentiation and results.

For example, while interviewing PR executives for this book, I came across an example of a very creative PR event for a Fortune 1000 company, costing about $50,000, which was able to generate over $13M in revenue. The creativity here was a significant driving factor in generating that kind of returns. In business-to-business marketing, the returns can never be that astronomical, regardless of the level of creativity. In fact, many of the returns hover near a factor of three or four. That is, for every dollar invested in programs designed to generate leads for new customers $3.00 to $4.00 is generated in revenue. Unless the design was just awful, the level of return would probably only be marginally impacted. Even then, it wouldn't be clear whether the lower marginal return was due to the design or some other reason.

One of the potential criticisms of this book concerns the ability to forecast returns from a specific marketing program. Even simple direct mail campaigns can have a margin of error that will either provide a reasonable return or not. The only way to get around this is to stick a stake in the ground and see what happens. Using prior experience or referring to available literature to estimate the returns is perfectly valid (The Direct Marketing Associations' 2002 *Statistical Fact Book* provides some great reference material. Visit www.the-dma.org.) Certainly, for larger and more complex programs, marketing is expected to test its assumptions with trial programs before the program is rolled out in its entirety.

Finally, I have often been asked how to successfully make marketing accountable for revenue without making it directly responsible for it. Marketing is not responsible for managing the sales team and it never should be. Anyone who has managed a sales team knows that the sales team is always in flux. A good sales manager will have his top players, his good players, his new players who may become good or top players, and the rest. A good sales manager will quickly recognize those players who belong in "the rest" category and replace them with new players. As much as marketing would like to believe it is achievable, there is never a perfect environment with a sales team of only top-producing salespeople. The marketing executive has to deliver leads that turn into sales with this imperfect sales team and potentially with an imperfect sales management. In the end, it all still comes down to the numbers. Marketing has to deliver leads that generate revenue. Nothing less is acceptable.

Section 1 – Introduction

What is ROMI?

Who should read this book?

What's in it for me?

Why should I change what I'm doing?

CHAPTER 1

"There's no better way to go back to the well to get more money than using a language that the money people can understand."

What is ROMI?

Before I get into describing ROMI, I want to make certain that we are speaking the same language as to the definition of marketing.

Marketing is more than just advertising. It's more than just Marketing Communications (Marcom). Marketing stretches from the generation of interest to the closing of the sale. It includes Marketing Communications (which includes advertising), Product Marketing, Product Management, Channel Marketing and more. It is the holistic view of how to successfully take products and services to the market. The marketing people are not just the people who put the pretty wrapper around the piece of chocolate.

Marketing Expenditures Are Investments To Drive Future Revenue

So, what is Return on Marketing Investment (ROMI)?

"Of course I want to get a return on all my expenditures. Why wouldn't I?"

If this were true, then why are so many investments made where there is no expected return? Why are advertisements run so that we can simply 'get the word out?' Why do marketing executives change the logo just so they can 'put their mark on the company?' So that we can 're-position ourselves?'

> Marketing expenditures are often made, disconnected from sales. They are often made to 'get the word out' but not to drive revenue.

Why do we buy a machine if we aren't expecting to save money or do something we weren't able to do before and which will then lead to greater profits in the future? Why should expenditures in marketing be any different?

The problem with marketing expenditures is that so many of them are made without a clear goal in mind. They are made without the ability to measure their results and without a clear definition of their success (or failure). They are made with no clear connection between them and the goal of generating more sales. They are simply made with the hope that more sales will come in the future. Often they are made because the marketing people want an ad that makes them look good. They want a product slick that simply shows off their design and creative talents.

Marketing expenditures must be made with a clear goal in mind, a goal that supports the financial goals of the company. That goal could be driving more revenue, generating brand recognition or preparing the company for an IPO[1]. Marketing expenditures are investments that will lead to future sales.

The Elements Of ROMI

Similar to other investment decisions, investment or expenditure decisions in marketing must consider four basic elements:

- o   Expenditure or investment
- o   Returns
- o   Risks
- o   Hurdle rates

As with any investment, the projected results (returns minus costs) must exceed a certain investment hurdle rate for a given level of risk. The difficulty of comparing investments in marketing with other more operational investments is that marketing investments lead to more sales. Compared with other investments that generate exactly the same profits, investments that generate higher revenue are more highly valued than those generating the same level of profit through reduced costs. Which would you rather have: lower cost or higher revenue? Given the current investment climate, any CEO, and for that matter any investor would prefer revenue growth to achieve higher profit versus achieving the same higher profit level at constant revenue.

---

[1] IPO – Initial Public Offering.

ROMI DEFINED

ROMI is defined as the revenue[2] (or margin) generated by a marketing program divided by the cost of that program at a given risk level.

The ROMI hurdle rate is defined as the minimum acceptable, expected return of a marketing program at a given level of risk.

SAMPLE ROMI CALCULATIONS

If a relatively low-risk marketing program costs $1M and generates $5M in new revenue, that program has a ROMI of 5.0.

If a company has a marketing budget of $5M and needs to generate $20M in revenue, then the ROMI hurdle rate for any low-risk marketing program is 4.0. This means that any marketing program must generate at a minimum $4.00 in revenue for every $1.00 in marketing expenditure. The example above surpasses the ROMI hurdle rate and is therefore an acceptable marketing program.

---

[2] It will be discussed later in the book whether revenue or margin are the proper variables to use to calculate ROMI. However, to simplify the ROMI calculation, revenue can often be used as a good proxy for margin.

Sample ROMI Hurdle Rates	
Startup software provider in first year of business	1.1
An established mid-sized, family owned construction services provider	5.2
An established mid-tier Internet services provider	3.0

Table 1: This table provides examples of actual ROMI hurdle rates for three different types of companies. They represent the minimum expected rate of return on marketing investments to generate new revenue across all programs at low risk.

ROMI is a tool to help yield more out of marketing. This tool, this way of thinking, will help the marketing team to conceptualize marketing programs, plan and budget them, communicate their goals and objectives, set priorities, gain approval, execute and manage them, monitor and measure them and, when successful, go back to the well for more money to scale them for even more success.

THE BENEFITS OF ROMI

ROMI is a language to help

- Conceptualize
- Plan and budget
- Communicate
- Prioritize
- Gain approval
- Execute and manage
- Monitor and measure

marketing programs in terms the entire executive team can understand. With these tools, you can now easily go back to the well for more money to scale up successful programs.

Marketing professionals, junior and senior, must start thinking of their activities as being one of the most significant ways to drive revenue. If investments in marketing are not providing significantly greater returns than investments in sales, then why spend the money? Why not take the same money and hire more salespeople?

Every marketing activity must show that it provides a significantly greater return than taking that same money and investing it elsewhere. In tough times (and they are always tough), it is even more important, as marketing departments are fighting for every budget dollar allocation against every other department. ROMI provides a no-nonsense, bottom-line basis for

> Investments in marketing must yield significantly greater returns than taking the same money and investing it in more sales personnel.

planning and prioritizing marketing activities. ROMI shows the success rates of marketing activities in a language that everyone can understand.

CHAPTER 2

"Don't forget you have to market the marketing department."

Who should read this book?

This book was written based on experiences gathered selling and marketing for business-to-business (B2B) companies, whether they provide high tech, low tech or no tech products or services, or otherwise. It is targeted at professionals in marketing but also in sales management, as well as all C-level executives, investors, directors and venture capitalists. Just as it can help marketing professionals communicate what's going on in their activities, it's also a way for the CEO or VP of Sales to tell marketing to go back to the drawing board when they come up with a plan to spend money on those overly expensive brand awareness campaigns that haven't been justified with a clear understanding of the programs' Return on Marketing Investment. It also helps the CFO nudge the less numbers-oriented marketing professionals to start putting numbers to their concepts.

The anecdotes and concepts illustrated in this book will provide the highest value for professionals working for small or mid-tier businesses. These businesses sell to other businesses for their internal consumption also known as B2B. Business units and divisions of Fortune companies may also fall into this sector.

ROMI will lead to more success which will improve the pocketbooks of those who count – you and your boss.

This sector should not be confused with companies selling to consumers, either directly (B2C) or through distribution, (B2B2C). Examples here include Proctor & Gamble and Ben & Jerry's. These concepts certainly apply to B2B2C and to B2C, but the anecdotes and examples may be less relevant.

The purpose is to help B2B executive teams make more effective decisions when managing their sales and marketing activities.

CHAPTER 3

"Yeah, but so many of my marketing programs fail. Do I really want everyone to see?"

What's in it for me?

"So why do I care about ROMI? Why wouldn't I want to keep hiding those failures like I always do?"

ROMI provides the ability to know when to increase your hit rate, to know when to invest more - or less - in planned activities and to keep proving your value to top management. When times get tough, you have a systematic methodology to re-align your priorities based on the new market parameters. You can be first in the 'keeper' line instead of the last.

When times are good, why not use ROMI and the illustration of the results of your efforts to achieve an increase in your raise and bonus? For the mid-level and entry-level marketers, if you are clearly showing that your efforts result in real revenue increases, you will stand out against those who can't. If you're not selling yourself, your accomplishments, or those of your department, you will not be looked upon in the same way as those who are.

At the senior level, ROMI is a tool allowing you to easily win those political skirmishes when you need to. To come out shining as opposed to coming out with your tail between your legs.

ROMI is a tool that allows you to come out shining when the budgeting process begins. In tough times it will allow you to be at the head of the keeper line instead of at the back.

This is no more evident than when the budget process begins and you can show unequivocally that your programs have provided a superior level of return and therefore, you are entitled to a bigger slice of the pie. Instead of investing in more salespeople, you can show that you need more money to run your programs. Not only are you making the salespeople more money, but you are also making their job easier. Even better, you're increasing the bonuses of those who count – you and your boss! (Or is it your boss and then you?)

CHAPTER 4

"Change is good."

Why should I change what I'm doing?

"Why should I change my ways to spend time figuring out ROMI?"

"Why should I spend my time and the company's resources trying to show that my activities generated sales as opposed to just leads?"

"I am trying to measure my results, but doing it is almost impossible because the salespeople just don't want to give me the data. Besides, not every marketing effort goes into increasing sales. Some of my activities are just to get a piece of literature out on some new products."

"And what about combined activities? Getting our brand out there is important. It makes all of my other activities really work but produces no return by itself. How do I measure the affect that one has on the other?"

The most difficult aspect of ROMI is to obtain the information you need out of sales. The higher paid the sales force, the more far-flung they are from corporate, the less they want to do for you. So how do you persuade the salespeople to give you the information you need to be able to prove the value of your programs? What's in it for them?

ROMI And The Sales Team

This is a simple question to answer – more effective marketing programs - but probably the most difficult to execute. Why should the salesperson take the extra 30 seconds to fill out the information you need to prove how well your marketing programs ran?

> In order to prove the value of your programs you need to get accurate and timely information on sales and what marketing activities lead to the generation of those sales.

What's in it for them is that they will get better programs. They will get more sales for less work. They will get higher commissions. Still a tough sell, but the smart marketing teams and the smart sales managers can get there. If you're still not receiving the information you need, you can employ rewards programs to obtain the information you need to measure the results of your work, to do a better job and to increase the value of your efforts to the company.

Some of these rewards can include:

- o   Tying compensation to accurate reporting (This works with moderate producers but only partially with top producers.)

o Tying lead quantity (and perhaps quality) to information quality[3]
o For top producers, I have had good luck with a simple *quid pro quo* offering. 'If you help me with the information I need, I will dedicate some direct marketing resources solely to your region.'

Changing the way sales and marketing work together to develop a clear picture of the results of marketing programs is critical. Without the help of sales, it is difficult (meaning more expensive) to obtain the results you need to justify your marketing programs, but it is even better to work closely with sales to develop programs that are really going to help them sell.

> Some Marketing activities are not done to generate leads, but to provide sales tools to make the sales team more effective. These have a very high ROMI.

ROMI And Sales Support Activities

Some marketing activities are not done to directly generate leads. They are done to support sales. These include activities, such as the development of sales tools or the development of collateral. These activities support sales but don't directly develop leads. They do, however, help to shorten the sales cycle.

---

[3] CRM (Customer Relationship Management) and SFA (Sales Force Automation) applications automate many of the lead and sales tracking activities. With a perfectly functioning implementation of CRM, the critical information that marketing needs is available. In addition, many of these applications on the market at the time of this writing have Campaign Manager Modules specifically developed to support marketing in tracking campaign results. However, many implementations of these applications have failed, because it is difficult to achieve a high level of quality and consistency in the data being entered. Even with these applications in place, it is often necessary to go back and sample the data in order to develop a clear and reliable picture of the results of marketing activities.

No one disagrees that every salesperson needs good collateral. How inefficient would the sales team be if there were no collateral at all?

The ROMI on collateral and sales tools is amazingly high and could be calculated based on the improvement they make in the sales process. The investment in good sales tools that support the sales process is not the issue. The issue is how much should be developed and of what quality. Is it possible to develop too much collateral? ROMI provides marketing the ability to determine more effectively how much collateral should be developed and in comparison with other marketing program investments.

USING ROMI TO CHOOSE BETWEEN MARKETING PROGRAMS

A software provider was trying to choose between a lead generation program and developing a case study as requested by the sales team in order to more effectively target a new vertical market.

Using ROMI as a way to compare the results of marketing programs, it was determined that the lead generation program had a ROMI of 4.5, that is, for every dollar invested in marketing there would be a return of $4.50 in revenue.

It was believed that the requested case study could shorten the sales cycle by 15% in about a third of the cases, by eliminating a sales call. The ROMI for the development of the case study was estimated to be 10.0, over double that of the lead generation program.

Using ROMI as a basis for comparing marketing programs, the case study was developed and the investment in the lead generation program was reduced to provide budget dollars for the case study and not go over budget.

Without ROMI, the marketing department would have only chosen to develop the lead generation program. The company would not have been able to reap the benefits in additional revenue through development of the case study.

This example illustrates the enormous impact marketing programs have on revenue. Tying the decision-making activities in marketing to their affect on revenue, as ROMI does, can improve the results for the company. Without ROMI as a basis for comparing these two marketing expenditures, marketing would not have the ability to make an informed decision between the two programs.

ROMI And Brand Awareness

In addition, what about those multi-million dollar branding campaigns that the agency always wants to do but can never tell you what level of revenue will be generated? How do you get the agency to give you some concrete numbers on the return on that investment? All you ever hear is "it depends on a lot of factors out of our control." Well, again, why not take the same money and invest it into more salespeople? They are directly under our control and we know that they can produce sales.

Brand awareness programs are typically very expensive and have only an indirect connection to revenue generation. They are higher in risk and afford less certainty as to their outcomes.

> ROMI provides a basis to plan and measure the results from your marketing efforts so you can make better choices as to where and how the company's marketing dollars are invested.

Nevertheless, the marketing executive must be able to choose between appropriate levels of spending with higher risk, more uncertain brand awareness campaigns versus other more direct, more certain, less risky marketing activities. ROMI provides that tool.

ROMI AND UNCERTAINTY

A hardware provider had planned on spending $1M on a print advertising campaign. It was also considering developing an inside telemarketing function to promote its new channel program. The expected cost of the telemarketing program was $1M. The telemarketing program was expected to generate roughly $6M in revenue in the first year, for a ROMI of 6.0.

Without using ROMI, the marketing department would have chosen the advertising campaign because it was felt it worked well in the past.

With ROMI, the marketing department was forced to look at how the advertising campaign would drive revenue. There was little expected return directly from the advertising campaign, though it was expected, but not guaranteed, that the program would improve sales through other marketing programs by 10%. The marketing team calculated this would also generate an additional $6M in revenue, yielding a ROMI of 6.0.

Given the higher level of risk and uncertainty associated with the advertising campaign, the telemarketing program was deemed to be a better, more certain investment.

ROMI is a tool providing clear decision criteria when choosing between higher risk, less certain programs and lower risk, more certain programs.

Section 2 - Marketing as an Investment

How do you determine the proper level of investment in marketing?

What is accountability in marketing?

How do you measure the return on less certain, higher risk programs?

How do you determine the ROMI hurdle rate for different kinds of marketing programs?

How does ROMI affect competitiveness?

CHAPTER 5

---

*"If I could only feel confident I was getting my money's
worth out of marketing."*

How do you determine the proper level of investment in marketing?

Marketing expenditures must be seen as an investment. Just like
any other program, whether the company needs to invest in
machinery, personnel or automation, each has a certain level of
return or hurdle rate that must be reached before the investment
project can catch the eye of the CEO. Investments in cost saving
machinery are typically made in one month with the expectation
there will be a return of some kind in the following months or
years. As defined earlier, the minimum rate of return acceptable
for a project is defined as the hurdle rate.

Investments in marketing programs should not be considered any
differently. If the company invests today in a new advertising
campaign, results are expected in following months. Whether it is

a direct marketing campaign or a brand awareness campaign, a marketing investment should lead to increased sales or a shorter sales cycle (which leads to increased sales).

Marketing Programs And Risk

However, there is also higher risk with marketing programs as they compare to other types of business investments. An investment of $100,000 in a machine that can produce widgets twice as fast as before has a clearly defined, relatively low risk with a clearly defined level of return. What is the risk of investing that same $100,000 in a new channel program that is supposed to sign up 50 new resellers over the next six months and bring in $2,000,000 in revenue this year and $4,000,000 next year?

> For the same level of profit impact, the CEO and investors would choose, at the same level of risk, higher revenue at higher profit over constant revenue at higher profit.

The risk is higher, since competitive reactions or other market factors may result from your marketing initiatives in the marketplace. The competition may copy your programs, slowing your ability to achieve results. Other players may announce new products or technology that may put your customers' decision cycles on hold. All of these would tend to reduce the certainty of your results.

With a simple investment in a new machine that can reduce costs, external forces are less likely to have an effect. The results are more certain. The company has more direct control over activities impacting revenue. Therefore, the expected returns must be higher for marketing programs in order to make up for their inherent higher risk versus other internally focused, less risky investments.

COMPARING INVESTMENTS IN MARKETING TO INVESTMENTS IN OPERATIONS

A software company had been able to maintain sales over the last 12 months with moderate but consistent growth. It had been distributing software on CD and was considering purchasing its own CD production equipment for a cost of $60,000. This was in contrast to the current method of purchasing the finished CDs from an outside service. Assuming that the company continued to sell at the current level, the investment in the new machine would yield added margin of $10,000 per month. If it was assumed that this machine would last 2 years, then the Return on Investment would be a factor of 4.0, that is, there will be $4.00 of savings for every dollar invested (24 months multiplied by $10,000 per month divided by $60,000 investment).

Summary:

Investment	$60,000
Cost savings/yr	$240,000
ROI/yr	4.0
Uncertainty	~0%

COMPARING INVESTMENTS IN MARKETING TO INVESTMENTS IN OPERATIONS (CONT'D)

The same software company was considering attending a larger, regional trade show and had budgeted $60,000 for the event. It was assumed about 250 leads would be generated and about 10% of those would close within 6 months for an average margin per customer of $10,000. This yielded a Return on Marketing Investment of 4.2, that is, $4.20 for every dollar invested in marketing (250 leads with a close rate of 10% at $10,000 per closed sale divided by $60,000). Unfortunately, it was feared, the competition would announce a very similar product at the show that would cut into sales generated through the trade show by up to 50%, potentially reducing the expected ROMI to only 2.1.

Summary:

Investment	$60,000
Lead gen.	250
Close rate	10%
Margin per close	$10,000
Total revenue	$250,000
ROMI	4.2 (w/o uncertainty)
Uncertainty	~50%
ROMI	~2.1 (w/ uncertainty)

Because of the uncertainties surrounding the trade show, the company decided to take a conservative approach and invest in the CD production equipment.

Using ROMI To Compare Marketing Programs

How should different types of marketing investments be rated against each other? Should the company spend more on reducing churn, increasing new customer wins or upselling/cross-selling? Often these are determined by many factors, including, for example:

- o Product life cycle status
- o The type of marketing program
- o Expected competitive reactions
- o Goals of the company, whether they are financial or otherwise (e.g., to generate revenue growth, be EBITDA[4] positive or be profitable)
- o The level of risk or uncertainty associated with the program

Just as with other types of investments, the primary deciding factor is the marketing hurdle rate that each program must be measured against. The marketing department, with the help of the controller, can determine these hurdle rates for different types of revenue generation programs (e.g., direct mail, telemarketing, email marketing, PR or advertising). Then, based on their relative risk, the ROMI for these programs can be determined and compared against each other to determine which programs are acceptable or not. This is the fundamental Return on Marketing Investment (ROMI) calculation.

---

[4] EBITDA – Earnings Before Interest, Taxes, Depreciation and Amortization

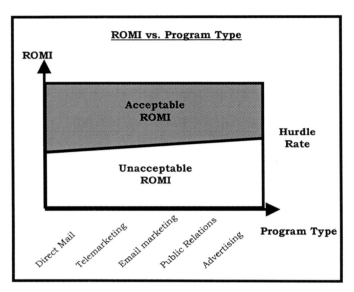

Figure 1: This chart illustrates the relationship between acceptable rates of return or ROMI versus types of marketing programs. For more risky programs, a higher hurdle rate is used. In this way, the viability of marketing programs with different levels of risk can be more easily compared against each other.

ROMI HURDLE RATES FOR DIFFERENT TYPES OF MARKETING PROGRAMS

A web services provider used a ROMI hurdle rate of 3.0 as its hurdle rate for all marketing investments. This meant that for every dollar invested (expended) in a particular marketing program it would deliver three dollars in additional revenue (return). In this case, the ROMI or hurdle rate was 3.0. Therefore, any marketing program that met the hurdle rate of 3.0 or higher would be in line with corporate financial objectives.

Actual ROMI hurdle rates for the web services provider, based on type of program, were:

MARKETING PROGRAM	HURDLE RATE
Customer acquisition	3.0
Cross-selling	2.5
Brand awareness	5.0

ROMI And Program Risk/Uncertainty

The ROMI for a particular investment can be calculated, but how do you factor in the cost of the unknowns? (Certainly, as CEO, we are all aware of the corollaries to Murphy's Law and in particular, no plan submitted by sales or marketing (or probably any department) ever comes in on time or on budget.) That doesn't mean the plans are bad and shouldn't be risked; it just means an additional risk factor must be added to the hurdle rate to account for these uncertainties. It also doesn't mean the sales and marketing teams aren't able to execute; it just means they don't have perfect foresight. It means marketing plans have risks, and the expected returns of those programs must be compared against each other based on the level of risk and uncertainty associated with that program.

ROMI AND PLANNING UNCERTAINTIES

A small electronics manufacturing company was determining its ROMI hurdle rate for the upcoming budget year. The marketing budget totaled $1M, and revenue generated from these expenditures was expected to be $5M. This yielded a base ROMI hurdle rate of 5.0. However, in the past, the marketing department has had a history of excessive optimism. For the year, the CEO decides to build in a planning contingency factor of 20% and sets the ROMI to 6.0 in order to account for this planning optimism, and also to account for typical planning uncertainties.

ROMI provides the ability to plan and compare marketing programs in the face of marketplace risks and uncertainties. Simple uncertainties might be, for example, variables in trying to estimate the close rates for hot, warm and cold leads over time.

Comparison of Telemarketing Program Close Rates – Hot			
	0 to 3 mo.	3 mo. to 6 mo.	> 6 mo.
Close Rates – Hot Leads - Estimated - Actual	 25% 21%	 15% 12%	 0% 4%

Table 2: This table illustrates sample closing rates for a telemarketing program. The estimated close rates were those used during the planning of the program. The actual close rates indicate what was achieved as the program unfolded over time. The telemarketing campaign lasted 3 months but directly generated revenue for another 6 months or so.

In order to account for these uncertainties and risks, the ROMI for this particular telemarketing program should be set higher than the minimum hurdle rate so that all programs on average can meet or exceed the planned ROMI hurdle rate. Especially for programs expected to have returns far into the future, the hurdle rate must be higher to accommodate the inevitable uncertainties in that future.

The more elusive uncertainties concern competitive actions taken in response to your program. Will the competition be willing or able to match your new channel program with a major awareness campaign that you just can't afford to compete against? Or will they simply ignore it because they have something else up their sleeve to grow their own revenue?

This is where the marketing team and the management team must have a firm grasp on all of the critical assumptions. Together they must be comfortable with the spreadsheet calculations underlying the ROMI calculation. Then, as the program is rolled out, these assumptions need to be closely monitored in case they are or aren't being met.

Every major new marketing program must be closely tracked. The more complex they are, the more variables there are that need to be tracked. The best plans must have contingency plans in place in case one or more of the assumptions do not pan out.

> Program complexity must be included as a factor in the hurdle rate. The higher the complexity of the program, the higher the required hurdle rate needed to compensate for the risk associated with that complexity.

For example, plan complexity must be included as a factor in the hurdle rate. For every level of complexity in the plan, the ROMI hurdle rate should go up. First, it is hardly ever true that all of the assumptions will ever come in as expected. Second, they will always come in later than expected and, finally, the more complex the plan, the more change there is in the sales team or in the organization or in the channel, and therefore the less likely the plans will execute in the assumed timeframe with the assumed results. It still doesn't mean that the plan should not be risked; it just means that the hurdle rate needs to be higher to account for the higher complexity and implicit higher risk.

COMPARING RISK FACTORS FOR MARKETING PROGRAMS

A construction products and services company put together a Risk Factor Comparison Table for their marketing activities in order to compare and determine risk levels for different types of marketing program.

Risk Factor Comparison for MarCom Programs

Risk Factor	Direct Mail	PR	Channel Program	Advertising	National Trade Show
Flexibility	High	Mid	Mid	Low	Low
Accountability	High	Low	High	Low	Low
Pilot Opportunity	High	Mid	High	Low	Low
Short Term Results	High	Mid	Mid	Low	Low
Results Uncertainty	Low	Mid	Mid	High	High
Fixed Cost	Low	Mid	Mid	High	High
Planning/Commitment Horizon	Short	Mid	Mid	Long	Long
Program Complexity	Low	Low	High	Low	Low
Resulting ROMI Risk Level	*Low*	*Mid*	*Mid*	*High*	*High*

Table 3: This table illustrates how risk levels for different types of marketing programs can be determined based on a compilation of different risk factors.

Ratings of risk levels may differ for different companies. Those companies with a clear track record of sales generation through advertising may set the ROMI risk level for advertising to be either medium or low. The same goes for any other program where prior experience can help to provide a higher level of comfort for the marketing executive in setting the risk levels for the particular marketing program.

Calculating ROMI With Fixed And Variable Costs

The ROMI calculation must include all relevant incremental or variable costs. In an ideal world, every program would include all incremental costs. Not just the costs coming out of the marketing budget, but, for new incremental revenue, additional sales commissions need to be paid, more invoices need to be processed, more credit card processing fees must be paid, in addition to the obvious expected Cost of Goods Sold/Gross Margin. Moreover, don't forget that as the program initially falters, there is always a temptation to offer some special promotions that weren't foreseen in the original plan.

> The ROMI calculation must include pertinent fixed and variable costs so that a consistent program evaluation can be made.

With a good controller on board, most of these costs can be based on some standard calculation, but often, when the entire sales process is being re-engineered, these costs need to be carefully scrutinized to make certain that all factors have been properly accounted for.

Indirect costs to apply to a particular program, especially for larger programs, include the fixed costs of the marketing department. This includes the full costs (compensation plus benefits, expenses and office space, if not included elsewhere) of the personnel dedicated to the execution of the program.

INCLUDING FIXED COSTS IN ROMI CALCULATION

A new program was being rolled out in the fourth quarter and would require about 50% of the time of the Channel Marketing Manager (CMM). His other duties would be spread among other members in the marketing team, so that no new hires would be necessary. The cost of the program was expected to be $275K. The revenue expectations of the program were $1,925K. Without including personnel costs, ROMI was 7.0.

Summary:

Program cost	$275K
Revenue	$1,925K
ROMI	7.0 (w/o CMM)

Including benefits, the cost of the Channel Marketing Manager amounted to $90K. Office space, travel and other expenses directly associated with the CMM amounted to about $10K. Including 50% of these additional costs of the CMM in the ROMI calculation reduced the ROMI to 5.9.

Summary:

CMM	$90K (fully loaded)
CMM expenses	$10K
Total CMM costs	$100K
Program related	$50K (50%)
Program costs	$325K (w/ CMM)
ROMI	5.9 (w/ CMM)

The costs of the VP of Marketing and other marketing overhead are spread proportionately over all programs. An exception to this might be specific programs expected to require disproportionate, high-level oversight. In this case, the ROMI calculation will need to include a proportion of these 'fixed' costs and, for larger programs, may even need to include office space costs and other fixed costs. These fixed costs, just like personnel costs, in most cases, should only be included in the calculation if the cost savings or increase will actually be changed or a personnel increase or decrease will actually take place to execute the plan.

The following table provides an example of how to use ROMI when developing the marketing communications plan for the year. The second table, labeled 'Marketing Planning at Full Cost', shows how to include the personnel costs of the marketing personnel as well as the overhead costs of the VP of Marketing. In this case, the marketing personnel are not assumed to be out of proportion to the level of marcom spending.

Sample Planning Chart for MarCom Programs				
Program	Cost (000s)	ROMI	Expected Return (000s)	Comments
Direct Mail	$150	3.7	$550	Even though the ROMI is lower than expected, the results have been consistent in the past.
E-Mail	$100	4.5	$450	
Telemarketing	$400	7.0	$2,800	
Direct Response Advertising	$800	6.0	$4,800	
Web Advertising including Search Engine Campaigns	$200	8.5	$1,700	
Regional Trade Shows	$100	8.0	$800	
National Trade Show	$175	3.0	$525	Even though the ROMI is lower than expected, the results have been consistent for the last 2 years.
Brand Awareness Campaign	$500	2.5	$1,250	Because of the high uncertainty and low expected returns, this program was stricken from the MarCom plan for the company.
Total w/ Brand Awareness Campaign	$2,425	5.3	$12,875	
Total w/o Brand Awareness	$1,925	6.0	$11,625	With this plan, there is an acceptable margin of error of ~16% and spending is under budget.

Table 4: Based on the corporate revenue goals, marketing has been charged with developing and executing programs that will deliver at least $10M in revenue from new customers. The marketing programs budget is $2M, yielding a minimum ROMI hurdle rate of 5.0 across all programs. As the example shows, marketing must plan and choose from a mix of different programs at different levels of risk and return to achieve the planned corporate revenue targets.

Marketing Planning at Full Cost				
Program	Cost (000s)	ROMI	Expected Return (000s)	Comments
Total (from above) w/o Brand Awareness	$1,925	6.0	$11,625	
Marketing Personnel Costs	$500	N/A	N/A	Costs include VP Marketing and all marketing personnel, travel, etc.
Total Marketing Costs, incl. Personnel	$2,425	4.8	$11,625	

Table 5: In this case, the entire marketing budget is $2.5M. Therefore, on a full cost basis, including personnel costs (and travel, etc.), the ROMI for marketing is 4.8.

Clearly, every company is different, but every company is looking for every nickel spent in marketing to affect sales in a positive way. Moreover, every company is trying to do this in a way that leads to increased revenue at the least cost at a reasonable risk.

ROMI is a tool quickly providing insight into how marketing programs stack up against each other in terms of investment return and risk. In addition, it can make certain that the marketing plans can deliver on the revenue goals of the company at an acceptable risk.

CHAPTER 6

---

*"Accountability - If your marketing department ain't givin'
it to you, you need to get a new marketing department."*

What is accountability in marketing?

To monitor and then to take measures to mitigate risk, the whole
management team must be able to track the progress of major new
marketing programs. Accurate tracking of results provides a way
to quickly pull the plug if the program is not working. However, it
also allows the management team to adjust the program as it is
progressing to make certain that the program has the best chances
of succeeding. Moreover, as the program unfolds two weeks or
two months into the program, the team as a whole is that much
smarter, so there must be room for flexibility to take advantage of
any newfound wisdom. Although there is always a tendency to be
quick on the trigger, especially for larger marketing programs, the
management team must be able to make the best-informed
decisions possible. Finally, knowing which programs provided the
best results or the most consistent results the previous year is

critical to achieving higher ROMIs when planning for the following year. This is where accountability in marketing comes in.

> ## TRACKING AND FLEXIBILITY IMPROVE RESULTS
>
> A mobile device software company was targeting the retail segment. Initial results in the first segment were slow to develop. Within the first three weeks, less than 1% of the prospect list was yielding any interest. In addition, those prospects who were interested needed additional product features in order to fully meet their requirements. To properly deliver on these new features, another four months of development and testing time would have been required. Before more time and effort were expended, a second segment was investigated. The level of interest found in the second segment after only two weeks was over 5% and this segment required no additional product features.

Accountability is key to continually improving ROMI. With a sufficiently capable tracking system in place:

Tracking program results and the underlying assumptions as the program unfolds is critical to achieving success.

- o Decisions concerning the progress of the marketing program can be made.
- o Future marketing decisions can be made based on the results of prior marketing programs.
- o Existing programs can be logically expanded or contracted based on real results.

It is not only important to keep track of the results, it is important to track the underlying assumptions that drive the model as the program unfolds.

DETERMINING THE RESULTS OF PLANNING ASSUMPTIONS

An office services company was rolling out a new channel program. Several key assumptions were made, some of which were tested in the early phases:

- Each telemarketer would average 80 dials per day and generate four leads per day.
- Each inside sales person would sign up three resellers per month.

Under these assumptions and the revenue per sale (not shown here), the program would generate a ROMI of 8.0.

As the program unfolded, the telemarketing team was generating only 72 calls per day but developed, on average, 4.8 leads per day. Combined this would have increased the ROMI by 20%, to 9.6.

Unfortunately, in the first two months, the internal channel sales team was only able to sign up 2.4 resellers per salesperson in the first month, 20% less than plan. This reduced the ROMI to 7.7.

> ### DETERMINING THE RESULTS OF PLANNING ASSUMPTIONS (CONT'D)
>
> At the end of the second month, further channel sales training was provided to help improve the impact of the channel sales team. In addition, the channel sales manager and the marketing team began working closely to determine what the objections were to the program and made modifications to further increase the reseller sign-up rate to 3.1 by the end of the fourth month. This yielded a ROMI of 9.9.

This example shows how important it is to be able to track not only the results, but to quickly take action when certain assumptions are not met and goals not achieved.

ROMI For Complex Marketing Programs

How can the company track a program's impact when the marketing program may begin to roll out in Month One and the first sale may only be realized in Month Six – especially when other programs overlap with each other during this time? Especially critical for products or services with long sales cycles, tracking systems that can follow the results of parallel programs from their inception through to their completion are necessary. Many Sales Force Automation (SFA) tools offer this capability.

TRACKING RESULTS OF OVERLAPPING MARKETING PROGRAMS

During the course of the rollout of the above channel and telemarketing program, it was decided to test a direct mail campaign to see if it would generate leads on its own and potentially increase the impact of the telemarketing campaign. For leads generated directly from the direct mail campaign, the ROMI was 4.1. Not only was the program able to generate leads directly, it was also able to increase the lead generation rates for the telemarketers where the programs overlapped. The increased lead rates from the overlapping segments for the telemarketers increased from 4.8 per day to 5.1. This was a great side benefit, but was not enough to justify the added cost of running a direct mail campaign to the entire telemarketing list.

Direct mail was not continued, since the ROMI for the direct mail campaign remained below the corporate ROMI hurdle rate.

If a business can categorize and follow a lead as it is generated by a particular marketing program, watch it as it flows through the pipeline and then the forecast, and, finally, recognize it as revenue – that is accountability in marketing at its finest.

DETAILED TRACKING IMPROVES RETURNS

The close rates on leads provided to the channel averaged 28% in the second month and 33% in the third month. By the fourth month, there were enough resellers signed up so that close rates between resellers could be compared. It quickly became clear that about 25% of the resellers had better close rates and that they were able to close the leads faster.

At this point, the lead distribution portion of the channel program was modified such that all resellers would be scored based on their closing rates and their sales cycles. Those resellers with the highest rankings were given more and more leads in their regions to further improve the ROMI. This had an additional impact on the ROMI of about 5%, but was expected to continue to improve the results of the program as the total number of signed-up resellers grew.

Only by clearly tracking, not only the sales but also the results of the underlying assumptions can sales and marketing put together truly effective programs with superior ROMIs. This is especially true for complex programs that affect the sales team, the channel and the marketing efforts.

CHAPTER 7

"Brand Awareness - We may have touched them but how
do we know if they're gonna' touch us?"

How do you measure the return on less certain, higher risk programs?

An added dimension to ROMI is exemplified by trying to determine the value and return from marketing activities that don't directly impact revenue. Brand awareness campaigns can certainly increase the returns of direct marketing and direct selling activities, shorten the sales cycle and increase the buzz in the marketplace. The value of the company in the eyes of the investor can also be enhanced. But what is the ROMI for a particular brand awareness campaign and how can marketing choose between spending $1M on brand awareness versus $1M on a direct mail campaign?

For the planning and conceptualization of marketing programs, brand awareness campaigns and other less certain or more risky marketing programs need to be planned so they generate a higher

ROMI than other less risky, more certain programs, such as direct
mail or telemarketing.

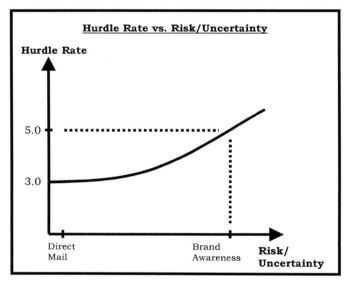

**Figure 2: More risky programs such as brand awareness must be designed
in such a way as to produce a higher ROMI versus other less risky
programs such as direct mail.**

Brand awareness campaigns affect every other marketing
campaign and sales activity. They improve the returns from direct
mail, direct response advertising and just about any other program.
In addition, they shorten the sales cycle and make the sales team
more effective. But by how much? Without clear and measurable
results, the impact is difficult to determine. That is why brand
awareness campaigns are considered more risky or less certain.
Brand awareness campaigns and less certain marketing campaigns
in general must therefore have a higher ROMI to account for these
uncertainties.

In addition, the relationship between more risky versus less risky
programs is a steep one, as illustrated in the diagram above. This

means brand awareness programs must be planned to produce significantly higher returns relative to more certain direct marketing programs, such as direct mail or telemarketing. A 10% higher return for a brand awareness campaign versus a direct mail campaign is not sufficient. If the company has had no way to track the results of prior brand awareness campaigns, then a factor of 50% to 100%, or higher, is a good start. Once there are measurable results as to the effects of the brand awareness campaign, this factor can be adjusted to more closely reflect actual results.

ANALOGY – ROMI AND RISK

An analogy of risk versus return comes from investments in the stock market. Investing in low risk stocks typically means lower potential returns. Utilities typically have very certain returns in terms of stock value appreciation and dividend payout. They have very low risk, but also have returns that are only slightly better than investing in Treasury bonds.

On the other hand, high tech companies are considered very risky. In the next twelve months, a high tech stock could be worth $200.00 per share or $2.00 per share. Because of the lower certainty and higher risk inherent in high tech stocks, the investor expects a higher overall return on his investment.

Investments in marketing need to be treated the same way.

With this added risk factor, ROMI allows the marketing executive to easily choose between competing marketing programs. If a direct mail campaign and a brand awareness campaign both are expected to cost $1M and each has a calculated ROMI of 10.0, the decision is easy. Marketing should invest in the direct mail campaign, because it can provide the same level of return at a much lower level of risk and uncertainty. The brand awareness campaign would have to provide a ROMI of at least one and half to two times the return of the direct mail campaign before it would be worth the risk.

Brand awareness campaigns do generate revenue directly, but their primary purpose is to help the sales team sell faster and make other marketing campaigns more effective. Many ad agencies profess that prospective customers must be 'touched' at least 7 times before the name of the company or product will be remembered. A brand awareness campaign is typically designed to facilitate these touches so that when the salesperson calls or the direct mail piece is received, the prospect has a higher propensity to buy.

> Brand awareness campaigns can generate revenue directly, but their primary purpose is to help the sales team sell faster and make other marketing programs more effective.

Every salesperson I know always complains, "We need to advertise in this publication and that trade rag and we'll certainly get some leads that we'll be able to close. Without these ads, not only will we have fewer leads, but also every customer we call will have never heard of the company or the product. We'll have to waste time developing credibility as opposed to spending our time selling."

There is certainly truth to this.

CALCULATING THE AFFECT OF BRAND AWARENESS ON MARKETING PROGRAMS

A startup selling a new software solution into the retail segment determined that the sales cycle was 90 to 120 days or about 30 to 60 days longer than projected. It was believed this was caused by lack of credibility of the startup among prospective customers. It was estimated that had there been credibility generated through a combined PR and advertising effort, the sales cycle would have been closer to initial projections of 60 to 90 days.

This differential in sales cycle meant that a brand awareness campaign could have improved the sales cycle by 25% to 33%.

Since brand awareness campaigns affect all marketing campaigns, these affects must be added to the direct return of sales generated by the brand awareness campaigns themselves. An example of this is shown below.

Impact of Brand Awareness Campaign				
Program	**Cost (000s)**	**Expected Sales w/o Brand Awareness (000s)**	**Expected Sales W/ Brand Awareness (000s)**	**Comments**
Brand Awareness through Print Advertising	$5,000	$0	$3,000	
Direct Mail Campaigns	$500	$3,000	$3,500	ROMI increases from 6.0 to 7.0.
Telemarketing	$750	$4,000	$5,000	ROMI increases from 6.0 to 6.7.
Sales Impact	N/A	$5,000	$10,000	The sales team can close more deals and close deals faster, increasing revenue over the period.
Other Marketing Programs	$5,000	$15,000	$20,000	All marketing programs will be positively impacted.
Total Incremental Sales from Brand Awareness			$20,000	ROMI on Brand Awareness Campaign is 4.0.

Table 6: **Because of the combined effects of a brand awareness campaign, even though the campaign will generate revenue directly, it also has a positive impact on other campaigns, including the ability for the sales team to close more or close faster.**

Other factors affecting the risk level of these marketing programs is the inability to test them ahead of time and the inability to modify them as they are rolled out. With most brand awareness campaigns, there is no going back after a start-up. Advertising space is committed months in advance and then it takes a number of months before the affects or the campaign can be adequately determined. These campaigns are also typically the largest cost item in the marketing budget. Programs that have these characteristics are therefore higher risk and therefore must achieve a higher ROMI versus other programs.

TRADE SHOW PARTICIPATION AS AN EXAMPLE OF MARKETING PROGRAM RISK

A small electronics manufacturer was reviewing its level of participation at a national trade show. In the past the cost of each un-qualified or even partially qualified lead was three times the cost of a similarly qualified lead generated through small regional trade shows. The decision to double the booth size for improved location was being considered.

Risks and uncertainties associated with the level of participation included:

- Unknown close rates of national trade show leads versus leads from other sources
- Availability of new products that might have broader appeal for the broader audience of the national trade show
- Cost control for travel related expenses
- Booth traffic flows of various locations and their impact on lead quality and quantity

Based on the risks associated with the trade show, it was decided not to increase booth size.

Not only is there a high uncertainty in the results of participation at the trade show, but there is also a commitment of resources far into the future. In addition, there is no way to test, ahead of time, the results of different trade show-related activities that might be able to reduce the uncertainty. Each of these factors means that the returns from the show must be higher when compared with returns from more direct marketing activities.

Non-Revenue Value Of Brand Awareness

Is there other non-revenue value associated with brand awareness? What is the value to your investors if you have a steady stream of good press published about your company? Venture capitalists certainly will value the company higher. Investment analysts also tend to value the company's stock higher based on the quantity of trade press the company has received and the name recognition

> Brand awareness campaigns can increase the preceived value of the company in the eyes of the investor.

the company has in its particular target segment. There is a perception among investors and investment analysts that this brand awareness translates into brand equity and therefore tends to reduce the risk for the company's future. For small and mid-tier companies, this type of brand awareness translates into a higher perceived value of the company; therefore, ROMI needs to be modified to include this type of value.[5]

Brand Awareness And The Value Of A Touch

Certainly, brand awareness has an affect on revenue, but what is the value of increased revenue for each of these touches and does one type of 'touch' have more value (in terms of more revenue) versus other kinds of touches?

At one end of the spectrum, lead generation campaigns, such as direct mail, have a relatively easily quantifiable cost associated

---

[5] It would have the affect of lowering the hurdle rate for a particular marketing program. Since revenue growth is related to stock price, ROMI positively correlates with stock value. In the same vein, brand awareness also correlates with stock price. Thus, brand awareness campaigns would have the tendency to increase both revenue and stock value. It would be an interesting study to determine the correlation between brand awareness, revenue growth and stock price for high tech.

with each lead and each touch. In direct mail, the cost per piece is known, the cost of the suspect list is known, the response rate can be based on historical experience and the inbound sales qualification cost of each lead, along with potential fulfillment pieces, can be calculated. The expected response rate is the highest risk variable in the mix. In addition to immediate revenue, each of these direct marketing or lead generation programs generates one or more 'touches' to everyone who doesn't buy, and therefore generates additional brand awareness.

Advertising is at the other end of the spectrum. With advertising, the direct cost variables are known and include insertion costs, the ad development costs and the fulfillment costs. The circulation and subscriber base, or reach, is also known. The cost per touch, which can then be calculated as the total costs divided by the reach, is low and typically significantly lower than direct mail or other direct marketing activities. What is often unknown for first time or sporadic advertisers (and no agency will ever provide a good metric) is a reasonable estimate of the response rate from a particular ad campaign and how much revenue can be generated from the ad campaign. Marketing can't quantify expected results from advertising unless the company

> Brand awareness is generated every time the company 'touches' the customer, whether it is a sales call an advertisement in a trade publication or any other marketing communications activity.

has had experiential results or other bases to depend on. In just about every case, response will be generated, regardless of whether the ad had a direct call-to-action or not. Each of these touches may lead directly to sales or, for those that don't buy, indirectly to brand awareness that may eventually lead to sales through other programs.

Between these two ends of the spectrum lies PR. Whereas advertising is what we are saying about the company and the product, PR embodies what others are saying about the company and the product. This third party affect makes touches through PR significantly more valuable then simple advertising.

PR, Advertising and ROMI

PR agencies justify their expenditures by offering up Ad Value Equivalents (AVEs). Every column inch that was written has an advertising column inch equivalent for that particular publication or media. This assumes that the column inches of a press article have an equivalent value to an advertisement, when, in reality, they are significantly more valuable. Their value is multiplied through re-prints and web-page links to them from the company website, not to mention the increased value third party endorsements have on these activities.

Unfortunately, the press value is comparing itself to a wishy-washy number. Clearly, each one of these touches will make other direct marketing activities to this prospect base more effective. These touches increase the impact of all other programs. The ROMI for brand awareness programs must then include this as a factor.

PR EXPENDITURES AND RESULTS

A firm that provided professional engineering services embarked on a 12 month PR campaign to establish the founder as an expert in the industry through the trade press. The results from the brand awareness generated through the PR campaign were apparent in the ability to place articles in a number of vertical publications specifically targeting the founder's expertise. Each of these articles produced results in terms of highly qualified leads.

This PR campaign cost about $130K and produced seven articles, each generating on average 6.0 new leads directly from the published articles. Of these leads, 30% closed with a value of $65K, yielding a ROMI of 6.3.

In the example above, the engineering services provider was able to develop direct business out of a traditional brand awareness generation tool. In addition to the direct marketing value developed through this PR campaign, the engineering services provider was also able to generate brand awareness, which also had value over and above the direct marketing value of the leads generated.

Certainly, with good brand awareness, other marketing programs work better:

o   The response to coordinated direct marketing campaigns will be higher.
o   The number of sales calls required to close the business will be lower.
o   The number of inbound phone calls will be higher.

o Investors will value your company higher.
o You will get more trade press and analyst coverage.

Does this mean that each of my marketing programs will be incrementally improved, let's say by 10% or 20%?

If this is the case, it may be better to invest that same money into more direct marketing programs and less into advertising and put the increased sales in the bank. Through this comparison, the ROMI of brand awareness campaigns can be calculated to see whether they provide a better payoff versus direct marketing programs. Table 7 below illustrates the ROMI for a brand awareness campaign in terms of its impact on other programs.

PR and ROMI

PR drives revenue in a number of ways, some directly, but most indirectly. Most of the time, when marketers and executives think of PR, they think of brand awareness. However, PR does generate revenue directly in many ways. For example, for every published article, some prospects may call in to order the product. For every article posted on a website, a lead may click through to your website for further information. For every case study written, the sales cycle may be shortened. For every search engine submission or web cross-linking campaign, a prospect may become a customer who was otherwise not targeted through other means.

> Assuming Brand awareness campaigns improve the results of direct marketing efforts, ROMI can be used to determine whether a brand awareness campaign combined with direct marketing yields better results than a direct marketing campaign alone.

So how can PR answer the question, "Why should I invest in you when I can hire another one or two more salespeople for the same cost and generate revenue? More brand awareness doesn't put cash to the bottom line this quarter."

PR activities, however, can affect sales in three ways:

- o Direct – Leads are generated directly through these activities.
- o Indirect – Brand preference/awareness is improved, and the perception of expertise is enhanced.
- o Sales Support – The results can be used immediately to directly support the sales team in order to shorten the sales cycle.

Certainly PR strategy, messaging and positioning are also important but they are what drives these activities. The table below illustrates how some of the major PR activities can impact revenue.

PR Activities and Affects on Revenue		
PR Activity	**Component**	**Impact on ROMI**
Media & Analyst	Articles (Print, Radio, TV, Web)	Direct
	Contributed Articles	Indirect
	Product Reviews	
	3rd Party Whitepapers	
Customer	Testimonials	Sales support
	Case Studies	
	Article reprints	
Internal	Whitepapers	Sales support
	Newsletters	
	Web-site content	
	Presentations	
	Speeches	
Web	Search Engine Campaigns	Direct
	Cross-Linking	
Trade Shows, Events	Awards	Direct
	Event management	Indirect
Associations,	'Expert' Credibility	Indirect
Standards bodies,	Community Awareness	
Philanthropy		

Table 7: This table illustrates how PR supports sales and marketing activities, whether that is through lead generation or sales support or indirectly through building brand preference or awareness.

Negative Aspects Of PR And Advertising

On the downside, both PR and advertising (and to a much lesser extent, direct mail) can create a lot of response from unqualified, unwanted prospects. Each of these false prospects needs to be dealt with by sales and can actually hinder sales in contacting truly qualified prospects. In most cases, this effect is negligible, but if it is not possible to filter these out through the selection of the publications or lists, then the costs associated with unqualified, unwanted prospects must be added into the ROMI equation.

Brand Awareness Accuracy

Often, what is understood behind a brand may not correctly correspond to what the company intends to be understood behind the brand. For example, following a merger or acquisition the understanding of what a brand represents can become unclear. Will the acquiring company maintain the quality standards of the acquired company? How will the new company continue to provide service to the acquired company's customers?

PR and to some extent advertising can provide a plausible mechanism to increase the accuracy of the brand in the eyes of the prospect and the customer by providing consistent messaging and positive re-enforcement of key brand attributes.

The results of these activities can lead to fewer canceled or delayed orders, fewer unqualified prospects calling in to the company, and the mitigation of other potentially detrimental affects of inaccuracy in the brand.

Contributors to Brand Awareness

So, what contributes to brand awareness and how can the value of brand awareness be measured? Let's first define brand awareness as anything leading to a 'touch' of a customer, whether directly from activities of the company (e.g. advertising) or indirectly through activities of others touched directly by the company (e.g., PR or referrals). The primary examples of brand awareness generation tools are:

- o Advertising, in all forms, including all forms of web advertising
- o Direct marketing in all its forms (print, email, etc.)
- o Press, media and analyst coverage
- o Shelf space in retail
- o More sales, through references
- o Trade show participation, trade show hand-outs
- o The website, cross links and search engine submission campaigns
- o Partnerships
- o The channel
- o Sales and telemarketing calls
- o Customer service and technical support

Measuring ROMI for Brand Awareness Campaigns

Everything a company does in the marketplace adds to its brand awareness, but what is the ROMI for these expensive, indirect marketing programs?

Brand awareness campaigns have different ROMIs depending on the position of the company in the marketplace, the price of the solution being promoted and many other factors. It depends on the target market, whether it is selling to a particular vertical, Fortune 1000 company, or small business. Even the number of customers in your target market influences how best to achieve a certain level of brand awareness. In addition, it also depends on the position of the company in the marketplace *vis a vis* the competition.

Measuring and determining ROMI for brand awareness campaigns is difficult at best, but it is possible. If every lead generated is tracked to its source, the value of the brand awareness campaigns can at least be partially quantified. With larger campaigns, test marketing can be undertaken to validate the assumptions underlying the model. If test campaigns are not possible, results from actual campaigns must be quantified. Average closing cycles need to be monitored, lead sources tracked, press column inches need to be measured and certainly, revenue growth closely monitored.

The higher uncertainty associated with the returns from brand awareness campaigns can be mitigated by increasing the required plan ROMI hurdle rate.

During the planning process, applying a higher ROMI hurdle rate can accommodate a brand awareness plan with highly uncertain outcomes. Then by tracking results very closely as the brand awareness program and other programs unfold, returns from the brand awareness program can be measured. Tracking needs to start with response rates through telephone, email and the web, then any follow-on activity, until it leads to a resolution (win, loss or not yet decided) as the lead moves through the entire sales cycle.

Once initial results begin to come in from brand awareness campaigns, management can begin to estimate potential program results. With the added margin of error the higher hurdle rates provided for brand awareness campaigns, management can now more easily compare riskier programs against less risky programs. In this way, the combined results of the chosen marketing programs will yield the highest return possible at an appropriate risk level.

CHAPTER 8

"Some marketing programs are more equal than others."

How do you determine the ROMI hurdle rate for different kinds of marketing programs?

One of the first leading technology marketing companies I worked with that used ROMI religiously set its value of 3.0. This was a service-based company providing annual contracts for services with very low churn, meaning most contracts were renewed every year.

This was a good first start, but not quite good enough, because it ignored a number of critical questions. To begin with, it used the same ROMI for all types of projects, regardless of what they were trying to accomplish. And it was inconsistent in measuring the marketing costs that need to be included in the ROMI calculation.

So, what should be included in marketing program costs? Do credit card processing fees and sales commissions get included?

How do uncertainties in the program results planning affect the determination of the hurdle rate? How is the hurdle rate affected for programs that promote high margin products/services versus low margin products/services?

Certainly, in Business School, we are taught that any project with a sufficiently high Net Present Value[6] is one that should be invested in. Unfortunately, no one can see into the future to determine if a particular program is going to produce the desired results next month or next year, not to mention three years from now. In all likelihood, the plan will be reasonably accurate next month and less and less accurate as time goes on.

> The ROMI hurdle rate for the company represents a baseline for planning purposes so that effective and accurate execution of the marketing plans, on average meeting or exceeding this hurdle rate, will yield the planned revenue target.

Calculating The ROMI Hurdle Rate

In a typical US company, what can marketing do to affect sales this quarter and this year, versus next year? How easy is it to justify new marketing programs toward the end of the fiscal year that will certainly drive revenue next fiscal year but certainly lower EBITDA this year? Should all marketing programs therefore be run in the first quarter and with the hope that the company can reap

---

[6] Net Present Value (NPV) is certainly the decision support methodology of choice, but it does have its flaws. In the case where the program has its primary effects within six months of the investment, adding NPV doesn't affect the calculation that heavily, although it can certainly be used. With programs impacting revenue over a longer period, the uncertainties in the calculations for the out years typically outweigh the value the NPV might add to the decision-making mechanism. I am suggesting that the ROMI hurdle rate needs to have a number of risk and uncertainty factors added in. Maybe the cost of capital for the out-years under the NPV formula could also change to reflect these added risks and uncertainties.

the returns through the rest of the year to show improving EBITDA?

Hurdle rates need to be calculated based on these and many other factors.

SIMPLE HURDLE RATE CALCULATION

A software company was beginning the planning process and needed to determine its hurdle rate for the next plan year:

- The total marketing budget was 7% of revenue (at plan) with a plan revenue total of $100 million.
- New revenue with new customers was budgeted at 28% over the prior year.
- For simplicity, all product margins were assumed to be equal and there was no churn. (Sales would be able to maintain continued sales at prior year's levels with existing customers with little or no support from marketing.)

In this simple case, the budgeted ROMI was 4.0 for the year (28% divided by 7%). In other words, marketing programs bringing in four times the revenue with new customers would allow the company to make its target.

With this simple example, the ROMI hurdle rate for all programs was defined as the marketing expenditures driving new revenue with new customers. It was assumed the sales team would maintain all existing customers with no support from marketing required.

In the normal case, revenue for the year is driven by a number of factors:

o Revenue from existing customers
o Revenue from new customers, 'self-generated' by sales either directly or through referrals
o Revenue with new customers driven by marketing programs

Marketing activities must be budgeted and ROMI hurdle rates must be calculated accordingly for each revenue source listed above. For example, to maintain revenue with existing customers, marketing may have to invest in a newsletter or other support materials so that these customers are not won away by the competition.

Similarly, for self-generated sales, the sales team needs support materials in the same way they need support to generate sales from leads generated by marketing.

DETERMINING ROMI HURDLE RATE FOR WINNING NEW CUSTOMERS

A cafeteria food service provider with $100M in revenue had customers on a 3-year contract term with about 1/3 of all contracts coming up every third year. Disregarding the occasional bankruptcy, revenue from year to year once a customer was signed up is pretty consistent.

In order to renew the contracts for the 1/3 of the customers coming up for renewal, the marketing team had to put together some support materials. The renewal rate was 90%.

The growth plan for the company was to generate 10% new business for the upcoming year. Marketing had been tasked with generating a plan to support this revenue growth.

Given the contract terms, $66.7M of revenue required only minor support from the marketing department, since these contracts will run throughout the year.

Based on the company's history, 90% of the remaining $33.3M, or $30M in revenue would renew their contracts with some support from marketing, but mostly through the account manager who had been managing the accounts for the year.

DETERMINING ROMI HURDLE RATE FOR WINNING NEW CUSTOMERS (CONT'D)

This would leave marketing with the requirement to develop $13.0M in 'new' revenue. The budget for these activities was $4M, of which about $0.5M was required to support existing customers with various support materials, new menus and the like. The remaining $3.5M could be invested in increasing the retention rate above 90%, directly winning new customers, or increasing revenue per customer with new add-on products. Any of these programs had to surpass the ROMI hurdle rate of 3.7.

Summary:

Total revenue	$100M
Revenue up for renewal	$33.3M (1/3)
Typical renewal rate	90%
Churn (lost customers)	$3M (10%)
Desired revenue growth	$10M
Total 'new' revenue req'd	$13.0M
Total marketing budget	$4.0M
Budget to existing customers	
	$0.5M
Budget to win 'new' customers	
	$3.5M
ROMI hurdle rate	3.7
(for 'new' customer acquisition)	

Planning For Potential Miscues In Marketing

But what about all of those marketing programs that don't quite pan out? How do those affect the ROMI hurdle rate across all marketing programs? Shouldn't we target something higher, so as to absorb the ineffective programs? - Emphatically, yes!

From the example above, if marketing's track record was 25% flops, then the ROMI needs to be set to 5.0 to account for the programs that don't work.

Fixed Costs In Marketing

How do the fixed costs in marketing, representing 25% of the total marketing budget, typically salaries, benefits and office space, affect the hurdle rate? If the fixed costs in marketing are higher for one program versus another, they must be allocated appropriately. Depending on how the overall ROMI was originally calculated, these costs were either included or not. If for some reason fixed costs need to be included in the equation (For example, three new marketing professionals will be added to the team to execute the new program.), then the ROMI hurdle rate needs to be adjusted accordingly.

ROMI must include all incremental costs associated with marketing programs, including downstream costs, such as credit card charges specifically associated with the specific marketing program. These incremental costs need to include incremental personnel as well as

> The ROMI calculation for a particular program must include not only the program costs, but also the fixed costs associated with that program.

other direct costs associated with the incremental program.

Revenue Based ROMI vs. Margin Based ROMI

For many companies there is no difference in margin between product lines. In this case, the ROMI calculation can be simplified by using revenue only.

DETERMINING ROMI HURDLE RATES BASED ON CONTRIBUTION MARGIN

The $100M food services company from the previous example had significantly different margins for their two product lines:

- The Warm Meals product line had a margin of 70% and Cold Meals had a margin of 35%.
- Warm Meals represented only 10% of the planned revenue, with projected growth of 100% over prior year's revenue.
- Cold Meals represented 90% of the planned revenue with projected growth of 10%.
- The marketing budget, $7M, was split between the two products was 25% for Warm Meals and 75% for Cold Meals.

This yielded a ROMI hurdle rate (based on revenue) of 2.85 for Warm Meals and 1.71 for Cold Meals.

Summary Warm Meals (WM):

Total revenue	$100M
Rev. WM	$10M (10%)
Rev. growth (WM)	$5M (50%)
Mktg budget (WM)	$1.75M (25%)
ROMI (WM)	2.85

Summary Cold Meals (CM):

Total revenue	$100M
Rev. CM	$90M (90%)
Rev. growth (CM)	$9M (10%)
Mktg budget (CM)	$5.25M (75%)
ROMI (CM)	1.71

If the contribution margins differ significantly and it is the goal of the company to generate profit, then ROMI must be based on contribution margin or gross profit generated by the sale of the product. Based on margin contribution, the ROMI rates would then be 2.00 for Warm Meals and 0.60 for Cold Meals as illustrated in the methodology below. In cases where the company is looking strictly for revenue growth, for example, in high growth situations, or where investors are valuing revenue higher than margin, than revenue would be used to determine ROMI.

MARGIN-BASED CALCULATION METHODOLOGY

Summary Warm Meals (WM):

Total revenue	$100M
Rev. (WM)	$10M (10%)
Margin (WM)	$7M (70%)
Margin growth (WM)	$3.5M (50%)
Mktg budget (WM)	$1.75M (25%)
ROMI (WM)	2.00

Summary Cold Meals (CM):

Total revenue	$100M
Revenue (CM)	$90M (90%)
Margin (CM)	$31.5 (35%)
Margin growth (CM)	$3.15M (10%)
Mktg budget (CM)	$5.25M (75%)
ROMI (CM)	0.60

It certainly looks like the investment in marketing for Cold Meals is totally out of line with the expected returns in margin. If it is, however, the goal of the company, for stock valuation purposes, to drive more revenue than margins, then the ROMI calculation must be done based on revenue and not margin. Alternatively, if it is perceived that revenue from Cold Meals can provide other benefits, such as more revenue growth in the following years, then the ROMI hurdle rate for that product in this year can be lower versus other products.

COMPENSATING FOR FUTURE GROWTH OPPORTUNITIES

A mid-sized wire and cable manufacturer had a ROMI goal of 3.0 across all products. The company was a public company and had to still meet its financial goals in terms of revenue and profitability as it prepared for sales of its newly developed products for the following year. It was considered the number two player in the industry.

The marketing program planning was complicated by the launch of a new product that was not expected to generate any sales in the year of the launch yet would require a number of marketing efforts in preparation for sales in the following year. These efforts included collateral and sales tool development; press coverage and participation at a national trade show determined to be ideal for the launch of this product.

The ROMI on these programs for the year of the launch was zero. Because of the extremely long sales cycles in this segment, it was not expected that any sales would be generated in that year from these efforts. It was expected that 15% of the marketing budget would be dedicated to the launch of this product, while the remaining 85% would be spent on the promotion of existing products.

Because of the lack of any expected return from the marketing expenditures on this new product, the ROMI hurdle rate for marketing programs for the existing products had to be raised from 3.0 to 3.5.

As programs are ranked against each other and ranked against programs for various products, then ROMI allows more sound decisions as to the desirability of one program over another. Finally, since the results of the marketing programs must add up to the generation of the corporate revenue and profit goals, ROMI can be used to weigh the programs against each other to determine the proper marketing mix to meet those goals.

CHAPTER 9

"Rest assured if you don't want the competition to do it, they will."

How does ROMI affect competitiveness?

The competitive environment and certainly specific competitive actions will affect what your returns can or cannot be. As your programs are developed, the plans must be based on the particular competitive environment. That's pretty obvious. But what about planning for specific competitive actions against your marketing plan? The competition will either do nothing, do something, or, either A or B. They will do it either immediately or within three or six months, or whenever. Each of these competitive reactions and their timing can and will affect the results of your marketing efforts and must be put into the equation.

In business school, we learned to use some kind of expected return calculation based on the probabilities of one outcome versus another. This can be done if you have a grasp of the different probabilities. In most cases, the CEO would probably contend that this is not adequate. If the program can't survive in all scenarios, then it may be more worthwhile to go back to the drawing board and update the program plans. If the numbers work out going down one path but don't work down another path, rest assured that the path least desirable to you will be followed by your competition. They are just as smart and agile as you are. They are going to figure it out and will react in the one most detrimental way to affect your outcome. (At least if I were your CEO, this is how I would reason.)

> CEOs typically demand that marketing programs must have contingencies built in so that regardless of the competitive reaction the program will produce positive results.

Unfortunately, you have to go back to the drawing board to see if you can come up with a contingency plan for this one scenario that works. The bottom line is that every plan must give you sufficient ROMI. If it doesn't, you won't meet your revenue targets, and there goes your bonus.

The more difficult question is, what if the competition does something unforeseen, either in reaction to your program or as a totally separate initiative, but one that nevertheless impacts the outcome of your program? What if they lower their prices 60 days into your program and you're forced to match theirs in order to stay competitive?

ROMI and 'Sunk Costs'

In terms of your ROMI for the program, you're now hosed. You're nowhere near, where you planned to be as the project was in the planning phase. The bean counter types will demand, "Stop the program, save the money. We need to be EBITDA positive, so stop the program." At this point, your business school training finally pays off, and the answer is 'sunk costs'. All the expenditures made to date that are not refundable or in any other way recoverable are sunk costs. Now the question is, "What is the ROMI to any future expenses, versus the new expected returns?" The good news is you saved your spreadsheet, and it is a simple matter of making a few changes to the assumptions. Here, as in the cases above, you need to find which new expenses must be made in order to tweak the program in response to this particular competitive action. Most likely, you're okay, because the investments you made in organizational changes, in graphic design, etc., now fall into the sunk-cost category. Finally, in dropping the program, you may also incur closedown costs. You now have to let go of the team you just hired.

SUNK COSTS IN REACTION TO COMPETITIVE PRESSURES

The number two player in the wire and cable industry from the previous chapter (Compensating for Future Growth Opportunities) put together and began executing a major channel marketing program to win 100 new cable installers over the next 6 months. The strategy was based on providing on average 10% lower prices in terms of sign-up bonuses, other incentives and volume bonuses. Most of the expenditures were in the development of the materials and communications of the program to the installers. The ROMI planned for this program was calculated at 5.4 (calculation not shown here) and was calculated on a contribution margin basis.

SUNK COSTS IN REACTION TO COMPETITIVE PRESSURES (CONT'D)

Two months into the program, the market leader decided to react by announcing a 90 day special lowering prices 15% across the board. Although this was perceived as a short term reaction to this channel initiative, it had the effect of undercutting the program by 5%, nullifying one of the key advantages of the signup program.

The number two player had two options:

- Match the across-the-board price cuts
- Discontinue the program

Matching the price cuts would directly cut into margins by up to 30%, thereby reducing the ROMI to 3.8.

Discontinuing the program would have meant that sunk costs would have amounted to 78% of the total (calculation not shown here), thereby saving only 22% of the total expenditures. Until the competitive price announcement, the program was on track to meet and possibly exceed its target of 100 new installers. But because the program was only now beginning its third month, it had achieved only 21% of its signup target.

SUNK COSTS IN REACTION TO COMPETITIVE PRESSURES (CONT'D)

Because 78% of the program costs had been 'sunk', the decision to continue the program with an across-the-board 15% price cut meant that the ROMI would be 13.6. Although ROMI for the entire investment at the new pricing would be 3.8, by investing only 22% more of the initial plan investment at 30% lower margins to sign up 79% of the target installers, the ROMI for the remaining investment was very high. It was clear that continuing the program with reduced pricing was the only alternative.

Summary:

Original ROMI	5.4
ROMI (w/ 5% lower pricing, 30% lower margin)	3.8
Sunk costs	78%
Remaining spending	22%
Remaining sign up goal	79%
ROMI (for remaining marketing investment)	13.6

Competing With Different ROMI Hurdle Rates

What if the competition has a different ROMI hurdle rate than you do? How does this affect your ROMI?

This can happen based on the structure of the market but also can exist based on the strategy of the individual players. If in an established market, one player wants to grow significantly faster than the competition, it must invest heavily in both selling and marketing. In this case, this player has chosen an arbitrarily lower ROMI in order to gain market share at the expense of the other players. This is often the case for smaller competitors trying to take on the market leaders.

There are a number of scenarios where different ROMI hurdle rates between the players in a market can occur. A few of them are listed here. Each of these can be complicated by a number of factors including the level of maturity of the market:

- o A growing market with a new entrant
- o A mature market with several players relatively equal in size
- o An established market with one big player and a number of smaller players

ROMI FOR A NEW ENTRANT INTO A GROWING MARKET

A small startup software company was entering an existing market where there was one market leader. Its product provided performance enhancements that the market leader would not be able to provide for another 2 years. In this first critical year, the startup was not planning on generating positive cash flow or profits. On the other hand, the market leader, a public company, was expected to continue to generate profits and had a ROMI hurdle rate of 5.0. In order to enter the market and generate initial revenue, the small software company had to develop name recognition as well as generate leads. Because the small company had no existing customers, its entire marketing budget was targeted to generate revenue for new customers, yielding a ROMI hurdle rate of 1.0, not unusual for a startup.

In the following years, the ROMI hurdle rate for the startup would jump to 2.0 in the next year and 3.5 in the following year, but would not be close to that of the market leader.

During this first year, the market leader had a number of choices:

- Change software development priorities, provide this performance enhancement as early as possible and pre-announce availability.
- Develop and execute marketing programs to block entry by the startup into their customers

> ## ROMI FOR A NEW ENTRANT INTO A GROWING MARKET (CONT'D)
>
> - Stay the course and provide new features that would otherwise not be available from the startup for a number of years.
>
> The market leader decided that it was not possible to entirely block the startup from entering the market. Since revenue from the new features under development was calculated to be worth significantly more than potential lost revenue caused by the startup, the market leader therefore decided to stay the course with its development priorities. The market leader continued development of its original set of new features. In addition, several blocking programs were instituted to reduce the level of potential losses to the startup. These included aggressive spiff and incentive programs in the channel.
>
> In the short term, the overall ROMI of the market leader for these and other ongoing actions was reduced. In the medium term, the ROMI was expected to reach greater than 5.0, once the original set of new features were made available.

As illustrated by this example, it is not unusual for a new entrant into an established market, whether a startup or larger competitor, to have a significantly different ROMI expectation. For the incumbent player, ROMI is one way to evaluate the impact this new entrant will have and how it will need to respond. Its own financial strength may also play a role in its ultimate defense of its market.

ROMI FOR ESTABLISHED PLAYERS IN ESTABLISHED MARKETS

A local construction services market providing a commercial structural repair service was very competitive with many different providers. There was virtually no expected growth in the market. This market had five primary competitors with a few secondary competitors. None of the primary competitors had a decisive leadership position. All of the five primary competitors were profitable with varying levels of success.

One of the five players decided to invest heavily in the market in order to grow its position and become the dominant player. Its plan was to double its level of marketing investment to achieve 50% revenue increase, effectively reducing its ROMI hurdle rate by 50%. Within 2 months, the remaining four primary players had become aware of this change in strategy and decided on their own courses of action. Two of the competitors decided to increase their marketing spending in order not to lose market share, while the other remaining two competitors, not having the funding to significantly increase marketing spending, decided to ride out the storm.

Because the market size was not expected to increase (and neglecting the secondary players), the additional marketing spending meant that the ROMI for all players went down. The three players who increased their marketing spending achieved increased revenue, but at a lower return on their marketing dollars. Revenue went down for the two competitors who were not able to increase their spending, even though their marketing spending stayed the same.

> ## ROMI FOR ESTABLISHED PLAYERS IN ESTABLISHED MARKETS (CONT'D)
>
> At the end of the year, there were three primary competitors, a new tier of secondary competitors, and the remaining handful of now tertiary players. The weakened tier of secondary players was now ripe for acquisition.

ROMI provides a tool to evaluate what will happen in the marketplace between competitors expecting to spend at different levels. This example is also illustrative of what would happen when a big player increases its marketing spending, thereby reducing its ROMI in order to grow and take market share away from its smaller competitors. If the smaller players don't respond with higher marketing spending and correspondingly lower ROMI hurdle rates as well, they will end up falling behind.

In most competitive environments, regardless of the types of players in the market, most programs are going to almost always illicit a response from the competition. Since any response from a competitor will have the effect of reducing your returns, you need to account for this lower return either by raising the hurdle rate or by planning for lower returns from the outset.

This has implications for the financial changes often taking place with competitors in your market. If one of your competitors raises a major new round of funding, that funding can be used to grow their market position at the probable expense of your market position. For the marketing team, it has the implication that unless your funding is also increased, it will be more difficult for you to reach your revenue targets. Your programs will either have to be more effective (which is highly unlikely), or your ROMI will go down. Not only will it be highly unlikely that the company will meet its revenue targets, but you will also not make your bonus. For every significant change in financing or every new market entry, you need to immediately begin lobbying for increased marketing investment to improve the opportunity of the company to meet its revenue targets.

CHAPTER 10

"Not only do we have to segment our markets in many ways, we also have to segment how internal marketing works, as well."

How do marketing funds need to be split between different types of marketing programs?

Marketing programs can take many forms. Several categories are as follows:
- o   New customer acquisition
- o   Reducing churn/increasing customer retention
- o   Upselling existing customers
- o   Warm and cold lead maintenance
- o   Blocking the competition
- o   Test marketing

Different types of marketing goals require different hurdle rates, depending on the program objective. As the discussion concerning the hurdle rates for brand awareness programs indicates, different hurdle rates are required for the types of marketing objectives being sought. If uncertainty exists in the potential outcomes of the program, then the hurdle rates need to be higher, accordingly, to compensate for this uncertainty.

During the budgeting and planning process, setting out to determine the ROMI for each of these types of programs is critical to developing a credible marketing plan for the year. It allows the marketing executive to present each of the programs and their trade-offs in their best light. It allows the CEO to quickly grasp how you have set priorities between programs.

PLANNED SPENDING VS. ACTUAL MARKETING INVESTMENTS

The table below shows how one small construction services division of an $80M company made the split between planned spending and actual marketing investments as it pertained to those activities.

The division had approximately $10M in revenue and the marketing programs budget was set at $1M. It was expected that about 75% of the plan revenue would come from repeat business from existing customers or be self-generated by the sales force. Therefore, the division was given the mandate that ROMI for new customer acquisition marketing programs had to be greater than 3.0 but should strive for 4.0 on average. The ROMI guideline for brand awareness was also pre-determined by the company. Given the low competitive nature of this particular business, blocking the competition did not come into play. Because brand-awareness activities, such as print advertising, were uncertain, the only planned brand-awareness activity deemed worthwhile was attendance at a national trade show. The customer acquisition activities were primarily targeted at direct email campaigns, telemarketing and an aggressive channel program. Marketing programs for churn reduction and upselling of existing customers centered around the development of new service offerings promoted through newsletter and direct mail campaigns. A small drip program was set up to drip on warm and cold leads throughout the year.

Comparison of Marketing Spending by Type		
	Planned Spending	ROMI
Winning new customers	$625,000	4.0
Reducing churn	$50,000	3.5
Upselling existing customers	$175,000	3.5
Generating brand awareness	$50,000	7.0
Blocking the competition	$0	N/A
Maintaining warm & cold leads	$100,000	3.5
Overall	$1,000,000	3.8

Table 8: Marketing programs do more than generate leads for new customers. Programs must be developed to follow the life cycle of the customer with the company and must be compared against each other, so that overall short term and long term financial goals of the company are met.

The specific mix of how much went to one type of program versus another had to do with where the company wanted to be at the end of the year in terms of total revenue, growth in installed base and revenue per customer. The primary goal of the company was to win new customers. In this example, this was driven by a new service offering under development, that would be coming on line in the following year and would be used to upsell existing customers. Therefore, the same emphasis for marketing spending was on new customer growth as on increasing revenue per customer. This emphasis represented about 70% of the

Components of revenue are typically driven through 3 sources: repeat sales, self-generated sales by the sales force, which includes referrals, and new customer acquisition supported by marketing activities.

planned marketing spending. Once this new service offering became available in the next year, it was foreseen that the emphasis would shift to upselling existing customers.

Crossover In Marketing Programs

Marketing must also plan spending to accommodate crossover or overlap between programs. For example, if marketing dollars are being spent to drip on new customers and also nurture existing customers, this can have short-term pay-off in generating immediate revenue, but it will also have future pay-offs in allowing a larger base to spread the costs of other campaigns in the future. Although it may be uncertain, what the exact future campaign might be, the future upside is nevertheless there, and it can be used to more accurately determine returns from various campaigns.

With telemarketing, direct mail and other direct marketing activities, it is pretty easy to achieve marketing accountability. With good tracking and measurement systems, sales can be tracked back to the program generating the sale. For example, with integrated marketing programs, costs and returns are looked at as a whole to determine the ROMI for the integrated program.

Blocking The Competition

With many offerings, if the competitor is blocked out of an account, the account and its future revenue streams can be owned for years to come. Here the revenue side of the ROMI equation has to do with the minimization of lost revenue.

A blocking move affected in marketing can be done in a number of ways. In high tech, it usually has to do with pre-announcing features in order to match availability of the same feature from a competitor. This will pre-empt the customer from switching as they wait and see what both providers actually have to offer.

ROMI AND BLOCKING THE COMPETITION

A small competitor announced it now supported a market leading complementary product used by one third of the market. It was immediately available. Prior to the announcement, the market leader was not planning support in this area for the foreseeable future. Upon learning of the announcement and its potential impact on its future sales, the market leader decided to immediately announce future support for similar functionality with availability in 6 months. The market leader invested in a crash development program that cost roughly $200K.

The Product Marketing team of the market leader estimated if this support were not available within 6 months, about 50% of the customers would switch to the software from the smaller competitor. If this capability could be made available in the six-month timeframe, the market leader would only lose about 10% of its customers, representing about $10M in future sales. The ROMI for the market leader was estimated at 20.0 for making this product development switch, combined with the announcement of future availability of this new capability.

Trial Marketing Programs

How do trial marketing programs fit into the mix? Certainly, marketing must have the leeway to keep trying new and different types of programs that may or may not produce results. The level of testing must be in proportion to the expected return of the final program if the program were to be invested at in full. The example below shows how dedicating 10% to test aspects of the program can increase the ROMI 28%, from 5.8 to 7.4.

Test Marketing by Type, Segment and Call-to-Action				
	Call-to-Action A	Call-to-Action B	Estimated ROMI A	Estimated ROMI B
Telemarketing Segment: Accounting	3.0%	1.5%	6.0	3.0
Telemarketing Segment: Insurance	2.0%	2.5%	4.0	5.0
Direct Mail Segment: Accounting	1.5%	2.0%	4.5	6.0
Direct Mail Segment: Insurance	2.5%	3.5%	7.5	10.5

Table 9: By investing equally in all segments and all types and all call-to-actions, marketing yields an average ROMI of 5.8. Using 10% of program budget to test market in each of these segments and 90% to invest in only the top four areas (white) yields a ROMI of 7.4 or an increase of 28%.

Often there is no way to test the program ahead of time. You either have to run the entire program and see what happens or you decide not to do it. That's why CEOs typically hate advertising. You can't really test the results without shooting the whole wad. In other cases, there just isn't time to test every program. You just have to go on the judgment of the marketing team. In these cases, to keep your jobs, you either have to be very lucky or you have to track everything. If you track the important variables, you can often make changes as results come in to optimize the ongoing results.

Section 3 – Accountability & Measurement

What tools are required to provide real accountability?

How does marketing get feedback from sales, when it is seen as a waste of time?

What does it take to reach marketing Nirvana?

How does ROMI apply to the marketing team?

CHAPTER 11

"Without the right kind of tools, we would all be back in the dark ages."

What tools are required to provide real accountability?

ROMI is an important concept for supporting decisions in developing a marketing plan, but once the execution of the plan has begun, the results must be measured. Marketing seems to often be at a disadvantage, not only in terms of measuring results, but also in terms of tracking costs. Not only must marketing work closely with sales to monitor and track where each sale came from, but marketing executives must work closely with accounting to make certain that all of the marketing expenditures are properly coded against the corresponding projects. Since these projects change throughout the year, marketing, together with accounting, must have the flexibility to set up the right cost centers, project accounting methods and other infrastructure so marketing costs can be tracked by marketing program.

Just about every company I've been involved with typically has the obvious kinds of cost centers – trade shows, advertising, direct mail, etc. However, you also need to know:

- o How much did the agency spend on developing the direct mail piece?
- o What were the real printing, drop and execution costs for that particular campaign?
- o How much was spent on fulfillment?

For companies primarily concerned about monitoring margins and personnel costs, the concept of tracking marketing costs on a campaign-by-campaign basis is critical to being able to know how to plan in the future, monitor results and report back to the CEO that the programs are or are not paying off.

> Without assigning marketing costs to the proper cost centers or periods, it would be easy for the CEO to think that marketing spending is out of control.

Assigning Costs To The Proper Cost Centers

Problems in tracking costs for accountants is *de riguer*, yet for marketing types this can be difficult. There are two types of problems; one in assigning costs to the appropriate cost center and the other in assigning costs on an accrual basis instead of a cash basis.

Not splitting invoices from the advertising agencies into the amounts for the specific programs is a good example of the first type of problem. For example, instead of coding all of an $189K invoice to the advertising cost center, this needs to be split $125K to advertising, $27K to direct mail and $37K to collateral development.

Using Accrual Based Accounting For Marketing Expenses

The second problem is more difficult and concerns the setting up of pre-paid expense asset accounts for deposits for future marketing activities. This makes certain that accounting can provide accurate costs for calculating ROMI for marketing programs at the end of the year.

CASH BASIS VS. ACCRUAL ACCOUNTING AND MARKETING

A small electronics company had not been accruing for marketing costs. Instead, the expenditures were being accounted for on a cash basis. This meant, that as the money was spent, the expenditure was shown as an expense in that period.

The company attended one national trade show per year. It was expected that a few new products would be available in the year, and therefore it was decided to double the size of the booth. This effectively doubled the required deposit. The deposit to reserve the desired location, which is normally paid a year in advance, was shown as an expense. Because the deposit represented more than the entire marketing budget for the month, the marketing department was unable to execute any programs in that month without going over budget. In addition, programs for the following month were dropped from the plan in order to make up for the budget overage from the prior month.

Cash Basis vs. Accrual Accounting and Marketing (cont'd)

In the following two months, the sales team couldn't understand why there weren't any leads being generated out of marketing. The VP of Marketing had his hands tied because of the budget constraint. Sales suffered because there were little to no leads generated. Revenue for the quarter suffered because of the two weak months.

The problem was quickly resolved by accounting for marketing expenses on an accrual basis. Because of this simple change in accounting policy, marketing was able to improve its planning, leads were generated on a more consistent basis and the marketing budget was not exceeded.

Tracking Revenue By Marketing Program

The other side of the ROMI calculation has to do with tracking actual sales by marketing program. In a more complex selling environment, it is important to track

- o   Actual sales
- o   Sales pipeline - all of the active leads with a tentative valuation
- o   Sales Forecast - the pipeline weighted by a reasonable probability of closing

Tracking the sales pipeline and forecast early on during the roll-out of a new marketing program can give an early indication of potential problems that need to be resolved before the program can meet objectives.

Other activities, such as activity by region, by salesperson, collection rates and many others, can be tracked as necessary to gain early indication of the results of marketing programs so as to adjust and tweak them if necessary. Many of this same tracking information can also be used by the Sales Manager to assist in managing the sales team (and potentially the telemarketing team). Most Sales Force Automation (SFA) tools provide these capabilities.

TRACKING THE EFFECTS OF MARKETING ON SALES

A web services provider was rolling out a new channel program. The Sales Force Automation Tool was put in place to track the activities of the telemarketing team, the inside sales team and the channel. After the first six weeks of the rollout, there were three numbers that were tracked very carefully:

	Actual	Plan
Sales pipeline	$248K	$225K
Sales forecast	$150K	$110K
Actual sales	$ 6K	$ 25K

Based on the initial results, it was apparent that the sales results were behind original estimates, mostly due to longer than expected close cycles. As the program unfolded, the close cycles were closely monitored to help determine if the problem was only in the close cycle, or if there had been a problem with the quality of the list or of the lead qualification process.

ROMI And Tracking Costs

The cost of tracking and providing reasonably accurate metrics as to the ROMI for marketing programs must also be determined. There are many tools, such as CRM or SFA software applications, which can simplify and automate portions of this task. Sophisticated Internet companies have the advantage in that marketing programs are integrated into order entry at the website enabling direct, immediate and low-cost tracking of marketing programs.

Not only are there acquisition, implementation and maintenance costs associated with any marketing tracking and decision support tool, but there is also an ongoing data entry cost. This ongoing cost includes not only the cost of direct data entry people, but also the time it takes for the sales or marketing person to enter the data and generate the reports.

These costs are fixed costs, and generally impact every marketing program equally. Unless there is an inordinate amount of tracking required for a particularly complex marketing program, these costs are low and can simply be amortized across all marketing programs in the same way the costs of the VP of Marketing would be factored into the ROMI equation.

ROMI Over Time For New Products

ROMI changes over time, depending on where the product lies in its life cycle curve and other factors. For very new products that bring in little to no revenue, ROMI can be significantly less than 1.0. The chart below shows this relationship for early stage products.

For products that are just being launched, investments in marketing must be made with very uncertain returns. Not only are the early revenue expectations low, but the uncertainty is also very high. Since it is a new product in a new market the positioning, value proposition and other marketing elements may still be under test. The impact of any marketing program cannot yet be well predicted.

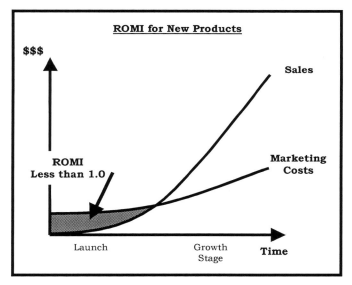

Figure 3: This chart shows how ROMI can change over time. For very new products where revenue has not quite begun, ROMI can be less than one, as the company spends heavily to win early customers.

As the product leaves the launch phase and enters the growth phase, ROMI is typically greater than one, but is low compared to the ROMI of other more established products.

This also has an affect on the competition. If you are competing against a competitor that is rolling out a new product, they may be looking at a very low ROMI compared to your more established ROMI. In order to protect your market position, you, too, may have to lower ROMI expectations and spend higher to achieve the same returns in this new, more competitive environment.

ROMI and Budgeting

At the end of the year, and especially as the budgets for the following year are being fought over, wouldn't it be great to go into the budgeting meetings and say "I beat my ROMI by 31.5%, and therefore I should get an even higher percentage of the budget for next year!"

As opposed to the plan ROMI, marketing needs to measure actual ROMI for all of its programs in the aggregate, both for the quarter and for the year. This will not only help the tweaking of ongoing programs, but will also prove invaluable for the ensuing quarterly and annual budget battles. With the ability to track how marketing performed against this metric, marketing now has the opportunity to potentially justify significant increases in investment without having to raise the ire of all of the other departments. With this yardstick, the entire management team can now see how well each of the expensive marketing programs benefited the company. Moreover, if these investments were good at the plan ROMI, they must have been great at the actual ROMI. (Of course, that assumes you were above plan.)

Tracking marketing results against a true metric and accounting for them properly can give the company the tools it needs to properly set budgets for marketing expenditures to meet sales goals.

With consistent reporting of marketing results by marketing program, tracking expenditures on an accrual basis instead of a cash basis, and tracking by program, you will begin to build credibility and continue to be able to justify planned expenditures and win the political battles based on factual results.

CHAPTER 12

"It takes too long to enter the source of that lead. Don't bother me!"

How does marketing get feedback from sales, when it is seen as a waste of time?

So why should the sales team provide data for a few more data fields? All marketing wants is the lead source and what happened to it. How can marketing turn this pain in the neck for the sales person into a value for the sales team?

Marketing is between a rock and a hard place. *"Not only does the sales team think that leads should be delivered up on a silver platter; they just don't understand why it takes so long to get some programs going that can really drive sales. Why don't they just run a good advertising campaign?"*

At this point, marketing needs to go into sales mode. What is the value to this internal customer (the sales team) of the information that marketing is trying to collect? *"Why should I take time away from my selling, which drives my commissions and my paycheck to enter that one additional piece of information into the database?"* It is certainly valuable to the marketing team to know how well a particular program did or didn't do. The CEO certainly needs to know. How does marketing get the message across that if there are more proven successful campaigns, marketing will be able to run even more programs to lead to even greater success?

This has been one of many of the problems associated with Customer Relationship Management (CRM) and Sales Force Automation (SFA) implementations. These software packages have become very sophisticated, but most of the

> Sales and marketing management must use carrots and sticks to get the information it needs to determine the effectivity of investments in marketing.

implementations have failed because of resistance in the sales force or the organization as a whole. It's a constant battle to get what the rest of the company needs out of a sales team that deems it a 'waste of time'. The typical sales concerns are:

- o "It will take me away from selling."
- o "It will give somebody else the credit for sales that I am trying to make."
- o "Other salespeople will steal my accounts."
- o "These contacts belong to me, not the company."

Nevertheless, *"We gotta have it. We need to do whatever it takes, including sticks and carrots, if that's what will give us the information we need."*

A Tiered Approach To Incentives

Initially, buy-in from the VP of Sales is critical for any detailed lead-tracking program to be successful. If the VP of Sales doesn't see that the marketing programs will be more effective through improved tracking, then the VP of Marketing has to first sell internally to the VP of Sales. Since a major share of the compensation of the VP of Sales is based on revenue generation, anything that can easily lead to higher sales should be an easy sell.

For the sales team, incentives can start with bonuses for accurate data entry. If necessary, reducing commission payout percentages for improperly entered data can also be employed. This can work for mid-tier and lower level salespeople, but may not work for the top-selling salespeople. Hiring sales support personnel to provide data entry and reporting, especially as a reward to the top-selling salespeople, can also be effective.

The marketing department can also impact salesperson data entry. Hiring a lead manager in the marketing department to provide lead distribution can also easily yield positive results. If the distribution of leads is based on salesperson data accuracy, then the sales team will realize that in order to receive more leads from marketing, the lead tracking information must be properly entered.

Other more expensive incentives may need to be employed. This is where the carrot comes into play: *"Enter the data that marketing needs and marketing will support more local marketing programs to support your region."*

In larger companies with larger sales forces, especially with a failed or marginally successful CRM implementation, it may be necessary to run a sample of the data. This can be done by either looking at the most recent sales or taking a random number of customers that have been won in the last six months and find out what marketing programs 'touched' these customers.

In the Internet or on-line marketing world, tracking the impact of marketing programs on sales is significantly easier. There are many software tools available that can directly track leads from websites or e-newsletters to sales.

PUTTING THE NUMBERS WITH THE PROGRAM

A software provider had been selling and marketing a software application to its customers for over 18 months. They had developed an ostensibly successful e-newsletter program, as well as a number of other web-based marketing activities that generated high 'open rates' and 'click-through' rates. Open rates for any of these electronic programs, where the newsletter recipient simply opened the newsletter, ranged between 33% and 45%. Click-through rates, where the recipient clicked a link that connected back to the website, ranged between 2.5% and 4.5%.

Although the company had a sophisticated Sales Force Automation tool, there was no clean and simple method to determine how many of these activities led to actual sales. Any of the customers may have received multiple e-newsletters and other pieces, but it was never investigated as to how these pieces caused the prospects to respond and purchase their software.

PUTTING THE NUMBERS WITH THE PROGRAM (CONT'D)

As an exercise, the company investigated all new customers won over the last 3 months. There were 47 customers. On average, these customers received three newsletters and two direct mail pieces.[7] The average time between 'first contact' from marketing and software purchase ranged from 48 days to nine months, with the average being 67 days. The average time between first sales contact and software purchase was 33 days.

Based on this investigation, ROMI for the e-newsletter was calculated to be 14.6. The ROMI for the other direct marketing pieces was 7.3.

---

[7] For purposes of this discussion, the press releases that went out during this period will be ignored.

CHAPTER 13

"What we really want is a dashboard of the progress of any program against plan."

What does it take to reach marketing Nirvana?

"Wouldn't it be great if we had a dashboard of all of the key components indicating the success or failure of any of the programs as they are unfolding?"

"Wouldn't it be great to see a real trend in sales based on any one particular marketing program? Wouldn't it be even better to cut your losses on a program before it's too late?"

"What I want to see is the drop date of a particular campaign, the status of follow-up calls, the forecast for any of the potential wins, the number of losses, the first closes and the estimated sales cycle compared against plan? That would be real marketing Nirvana."

Many of the Sales Force Automation tools can provide these types of information. Even though these tools aren't perfect, they can provide a great tracking mechanism to effectively monitor and manage programs with better results.

A DIGITAL DASHBOARD FOR MARKETING

To continue the example concerning the telemarketing/channel program from Chapter 11, the General Manager, the Director of Marketing and the Sales Manager needed to have one quick view of the status of the program at any moment during the day. The table below shows the information desired to monitor the success or failure of the new program.

Sample Digital Dashboard			
	Today	**Month To Date**	**Quarter To Date**
Telemarketing			
No. of dials	525	Ave. = 536	Ave. = 535
No. of leads generated	30.0	Ave. = 30.6	Ave. = 31.2
Lead percentage	5.7%	5.7%	5.8%
Sales			
Revenue	$48,000	$576,000	$2,406,000
New Customer Wins (rate %)	3 (27%)	9 (29%)	14 (25%)
Losses	8	22	41
No. of Dials	274	Ave. = 271	Ave. = 269
New Resellers	1	3	12
Current Pipeline	$7,130,000	$7,130,000	$7,130,000
Current Month Forecast	$1,450,000	$1,450,000	$1,450,000
Marketing			
Est. ROMI	N/A	5.5	5.7

Table 10: This sample dashboard was built to manage sales and marketing as well as report results back to corporate to show actual sales and ROMI as the program unfolded. This dashboard was made available to the General Manager, Director of Marketing and the Sales Manager.

Unfortunately, with many marketing programs it is not possible to determine early on whether these programs will be effective, so as to quickly make corrections or potentially pull the plug in order to save on failing marketing costs. Direct marketing programs such as telemarketing and direct mail do provide early results and indicators of success or failure, so it's possible to adjust them as they unfold. With brand awareness campaigns, all the money is often spent before the first phone call is answered or the first nickel of revenue has been recognized. In this case, the early indicators simply aren't early enough.

CHAPTER 14

"When times get tough, the marketing professional who spends more time talking about and delivering returns and revenue and less about colors and design deserves to be at the head of the 'keeper line.'"

How does ROMI apply to the marketing team?

How do we know we are getting all we can out of marketing? Isn't the company investing in each and every member of the marketing team, just like it is investing in specific marketing programs?

"Shouldn't I get a return on my investment out of every employee in marketing?"

Let's take what we've learned and apply it to the marketing team itself, because in the end it is up to that team to be a primary driver of the financial and strategic goals of the company. The marketing team is there to generate leads in a consistent and high-quality fashion to feed the sales team so they can close them.

ROMI FOR THE VP OF MARKETING

A small software company had three mid-level marketing professionals, each responsible for various aspects of the marketing department. Until recently they had been reporting directly to the CEO, but the CEO determined that it was now time to invest in a full-time VP of Marketing in order to take the company to the next level. The CEO had been spending about 1/3 of his time managing this group. For this size company, the VP of Marketing commanded a salary and bonus package of about $150,000 and some incentive stock options.

The VP of Marketing would be responsible for a budget of $1.5M to generate $10M in new revenue. The $1.5M in budget included spending on programs and on personnel.

The investment in the VP of Marketing had to generate a ROMI of 6.7, just like any other marketing investment.

Just as with any other marketing program or expenditure, the CEO or the VP of Marketing must trade off making one investment against making another. In this case, the company needs a ROMI of 6.7 out of the entire marketing department, including costs for each of the marketing professionals.

ROMI FOR THE VP OF MARKETING (CONT'D)

With the VP of Marketing now on board, the marketing department of the same software company had to generate a ROMI of 7.4 from programs alone. The programs had to be 10% more effective with the VP of Marketing than without[8].

Of course, the VP of Marketing has to do more than just generate a 10% improvement in the results of the marketing department; otherwise, why do it? The issue is that from a pure cost perspective, there is a certain minimum level of expectations that have to be met. From the perspective of the VP of Marketing, coming in to provide a 10% improvement over existing capabilities should be easy.

The marketing professional who understands that he or she will be judged based on his or her ability to generate leads that drive sales will be judged more favorably than someone that sees the end goal as a great-looking collateral piece.

Implications For Mid-Level Marketing Professionals

The same relationships apply to anyone in the marketing department, regardless of the level of responsibility. The cost invested in the marketing professional plays an important part of the equation in terms of

---

[8] To maintain simplicity, the opportunity cost of one third of the CEO's time was not included in the calculation. This would have the resultof reducing the increase.

how the company is going to recoup a return from the investment in the salary of that individual and the programs that are being managed by that individual.

This has implications for the type of individual who should be hired into any marketing position. A marketing professional who understands that his worth is being judged by his or her ability to drive leads that drive sales will be more sought after than an individual that sees the end goal as a great-looking collateral piece. Certainly, there is a lot of value in well-produced and designed materials, but if the goal of the piece is not to help drive sales, then the piece is superfluous, or it will totally miss the mark.

The first question from any marketing professional should always be *"How will this drive sales more than some other marketing activity?"*

> ROMI is a tool that can help you to keep your job when times get tough.

ROMI also helps you to keep your job when times get tough. What's more important to a company in bad times than driving revenue? If you have a proven track record and an ability to prove the results of your programs, then your prospects are good. If up until the downturn you have been producing and have proof that you can keep delivering, then your job may be safe.

Without these metrics in your bag, clearly illustrating how your programs have produced real returns, your chances are a lot lower that you can prove your worth when the ax comes swinging your way.

ROMI And The Interview Process

ROMI is also useful during the interview process. For those companies who aren't already using ROMI-based planning, you will have a lot to offer. However, you can also use ROMI as a tool to understand your chances for success with the new company. You will be able to validate whether the expectations the hiring company has for you are in line with the market.

UNDERSTANDING JOB EXPECTATIONS WITH ROMI

An electronics company was hiring a new VP of Marketing into a newly created position for the new fiscal year. The market segment served by the company was growing at a good rate, and all indications were that the market would continue to grow.

The marketing budget had been set to increase from $3.5M to $5.0M in the new year. The increased revenue budget driven by this marketing budget was increased from $14M to $19M. This represented an expected growth rate of 35%. The market was expected to grow at this rate as well, so the expectation was that the company would maintain its market share.

With this company, the marketing expenditures had to generate a ROMI of 3.8 in comparison with the prior year of 4.0. With all other things being equal, the job for the incoming VP of Marketing would actually have been easier than for his predecessor (the CEO).

Certainly, many other issues come into play, including the investments to be made in the sales team, as well as activities the competition will undertake. If, for example, the growth rate was to come solely from marketing in a stagnant market, without commensurate increases in investments in sales, this revenue target might not be achievable. If, on the other hand, the market is expected to double, and there are commensurate increases in the sales team, then these numbers would be easy to achieve.

ROMI is certainly not the only factor to consider when interviewing for a new position, but it does provide a way to determine whether the expectations of the hiring company are in line with the market and how that will affect your ability to achieve the goals you are signing up for.

Section 4 – Conclusion

Putting it all together

CHAPTER 15

"ROMI can allow you to go back to the well for more money."

Putting it all together

ROMI is a tool to help the marketing department, marketing professionals and the management team to maintain a tight connection between marketing programs – from conception through execution – and to drive revenue. It can help to answer the question of whether the company should invest more into one program versus another, or even one department versus another.

SETTING THE MARKETING BUDGET

In the beginning of the year, a software services company set the marketing budget for the new fiscal year to $3.5M with a sales target of $14M. The ROMI hurdle rate required to meet this objective was 4.0. The personnel and non-program costs were budgeted at $0.5M. The ROMI hurdle rate for programs was 4.7. For planning purposes, the VP of Marketing set the hurdle rate for marketing programs to 5.6, or 20% higher, in order to provide cushion for some marketing programs that may not pay-off as planned.

The company was planning to go public in the following year, so some of the marketing investments were planned to generate brand awareness among potential investors.

Table 10 shows an overview of the plan.

Low Risk Programs

The plan ROMI numbers for telemarketing, email marketing, web sales & marketing and direct mail are based on existing experience from prior years. These programs are assigned a low risk level based on past experience and their direct impact on influencing sales.

Moderate Risk Programs

The local trade shows were assumed to have moderate risk because of their direct affect on generating leads, but inconsistent success from show to show and from region to region. They can also be scheduled on short notice, so they don't represent unknowns far out into the future.

PR was assigned a moderate risk level because results have had a high pay-off in the past. The PR efforts of the company have

PR was considered a moderate-risk marketing activity because results were consistent and had a clearly higher value than advertising.

traditionally been very effective in generating a number of print articles on a quarterly basis. It is assumed that no direct revenue comes from any of these activities, even though there is anecdotal evidence to support this. As in the case of the national trade show and the advertising plans, it is assumed that the PR efforts will have a positive affect on all other programs and will improve them by an estimated 10%. Even though the results of PR efforts are predictable, due to the lack of a direct connection to sales and the inability to place an article consistently in the publications of choice, PR is assigned a moderate level of risk/uncertainty. It is not assigned a high level of risk since, based on past experience and the Ad Value Equivalent to print advertising, PR has provided a value of about 3.5 to one over advertising expenditures[9].

---

[9] Ad Value Equivalents or Column-inch Equivalents compare the number of column inches of print press coverage from articles written about the company to the cost of a print advertisement had the company paid for the same amount of space in the same publication. For example, if PR efforts generated one full page article on the company, this would be worth the same amount of print advertising. In a typical national technology trade publication, depending on circulation, a one page, single insertion rate advertisement might cost anywhere from $15,000 to $30,000. This is a reasonable proxy for the value of the article in dollars and sense, but doesn't tell the whole story, since a one page article written about the company has more value than a one-page advertisement.

Even though the PR activities only had a plan ROMI of 5.6, which would be too low for the level of risk, the spending level was approved because of the brand awareness value for the upcoming IPO.

High Risk Programs

The national trade show and the advertising plan were deemed to be high risk, because direct results have been sporadic in the past. In addition, these costs are fixed once the commitment has been made. It is difficult to turn them off due to the long lead times, so if events in the marketplace affect potential outcomes, there is little to no recourse to adjusting expenditures down (or up.) There is an expected positive brand awareness affect, so it is assumed that this brand awareness will affect all other programs by 10% each. In addition, the brand awareness generated through these programs will help in the IPO process.

> ## REVIEW OF PREVIOUS YEAR AND LOOKING AHEAD WITH ROMI
>
> It was now the end of the year and the company was looking to develop budgets for the following fiscal year. The VP of Marketing developed the following table (Table 11) of results of the marketing programs and compared it to the planned expenditures for the year.

Marketing Expenditures Plan – Current Fiscal Year				
Program	Expenditure - Plan	Revenue Impact - Plan	ROMI - Plan	Risk/ Uncertainty
Telemarketing: Lead Gen.	$175K	$1,750K	10.0	Low
Direct Mail: Cross-selling	$75K	$675K	9.0	Low
Email Marketing	$250K	$1,500K	6.0	Low
Web Sales & Marketing	$75K	$75K	10.0	Low
Direct Mail: Lead Gen.	$750K	$5,625K	7.5	Low
Local Trade Shows	$125K	$875K	7.0	Moderate
PR	$250K	$0K direct, $1,400K (10% of total not in totals)	5.6	Moderate
National Trade Show	$300K	$1,350K (direct revenue plus 10% of total as brand awareness value)	4.5 (direct, 9.2 including brand awareness value)	High
Advertising: Lead Gen.	$1,000K	$5,000 (direct revenue plus 10% of total as brand awareness value)	5.0 (direct, 6.4 including brand awareness value)	High
Budget	$3,000K	$16,850K	5.6	

Table 11: This table illustrates how the VP of Marketing and the management team assigned risk levels to each type of marketing program.

REVIEW OF PREVIOUS YEAR AND LOOKING AHEAD WITH ROMI

The plan from the prior year was compared to actual results accomplished throughout the year (Table 12). Actual ROMI was calculated and yielded an overall value of 5.8 in comparison with the plan ROMI of 4.7. This difference was due in part by investing over budget in programs that were very successful, such as, telemarketing, direct mail and local trade shows.

Marketing Results – Current Fiscal Year				
Program	**Expenditure - Actual**	**Revenue Impact - Actual**	**ROMI - Plan**	**ROMI - Actual**
Telemarketing: Lead Gen.	$400K (orig. budget $175K)	$3,200K	10.0	8.0
Direct Mail: Cross-selling	$150K (orig. budget $75K)	$1,500K	9.0	10.0
Email Marketing	$250K	$1,800K	6.0	7.2
Web Sales & Marketing	$75K	$1,050K	10.0	14.0
Direct Mail: Lead Gen.	$750K	$4,500K	7.5	6.0
Local Trade Shows	$350K (orig. budget 125K)	$1,995K	7.0	5.7
PR	$250K	$0K direct, $1,400K (10% of total) not in totals	5.6	5.6
National Trade Show	$300K	$750K (direct revenue plus 10% of total as brand awareness value)	4.5 (direct, 9.2 including brand awareness value)	2.5
Advertising: Lead Gen.	$1,000K	$1,000 (direct revenue plus 10% of total as brand awareness value)	5.0 (direct, 6.4 including brand awareness value)	1.0
Total	$3,525K	$15,750K	5.8	4.5
Plan	$3,000K	$14,000K	4.7	N/A

Table 12: Due to the higher than expected results from telemarketing, direct mail and local trade shows, the company invested over budget in these areas, to beat the plan revenue by 12.5%.

This example illustrates a number of activities that this VP of Marketing was able to undertake.

First and foremost, he was able to take advantage of opportunities that allowed him to go over budget but deliver higher than expected revenue. Based on early positive results, the telemarketing, direct mail and local trade show programs were expanded to generate additional revenue. The ROMIs were 8.0, 10.0 and 5.7, respectively. Overall, the marketing expenditures were over budget by $525K, but were able to deliver an additional $1.8M in revenue for a ROMI of 7.3 for these activities. If it were possible, further investments in Web Sales & Marketing would have yielded the best returns, but there were no good opportunities to increase this further with the same expected returns.

Because of higher than expected returns on direct marketing activities and lower than expected returns on indirect marketing activities, spending was increased on direct marketing programs to beat the revenue (and profit) target.

The biggest disappointments were the returns from the advertising and national trade show programs. The calculation of the plan ROMI for the advertising program was 5.0 for direct revenue, but 6.4 when considering the brand awareness value (10% of total sales). It was expected that the advertising program would generate $5.0M in revenue. With a ROMI of 6.4, the return was initially thought to be worth the risk, because of direct revenue generated and the brand awareness value for the upcoming IPO. The actual returns were 1.0, or $1.0M in revenue when considering only direct revenue, and 2.6 when considering a 10% brand awareness impact on total revenue. This is still too low to justify those expenditures on a revenue basis alone. For next year, market research and tracking budgets will be set aside to determine if the brand awareness value of the PR, national trade show and the advertising programs actually paid off and, potentially, whether they could be improved.

The national trade show plan ROMIs were 4.5 for direct revenue and 9.2 including the brand awareness value of 10% of total sales. Actual direct ROMI was 2.5 and the brand awareness value yielded 7.7 ROMI.

In summary, marketing was able to clearly show the management team the results of their plans to drive revenue, make trade-offs between programs and increase revenue over expectations at a cost and risk level acceptable to the management team.

Marketing expenditures were allowed to exceed the budget in order to make up for shortfalls due to the low direct results of the trade show and advertising expenditures.

Marketing must always plan and execute to generate revenue. Investments in marketing must always be connected to results in sales, whether it is this quarter, next quarter or beyond. Never forget the question *"Why should we spend that money on that marketing program? Why don't we just hire more salespeople?"*

Appendix

Sample ROMI Hurdle Rate Calculation Worksheet

This worksheet provides a basis to calculate ROMI Hurdle Rates for product lines, business units, divisions or the entire company for low, medium and high risk programs.

Sample ROMI Hurdle Rate Calculation Worksheet	
Activity/Step	**Your Numbers**

Entity:
    Product line
    Business unit
    Division
    Company-wide
    Other	

Step #1 Choose margin vs. revenue based ROMI calculation	
Step #2 Choose ROMI for programs only or programs and personnel costs	
Step #3 Planning Contingency Factor	

Step #4
    From the revenue (margin) plan, determine:
      a. Existing Customers: The revenue (margin) goal that will come from existing customers	

b. Self-Generation Sales Support: The revenue (margin) that will be self-generated by the sales force	
c. New Customer Acquisition: The revenue (margin) goal that will come from new sales to new customers	

Sample ROMI Hurdle Rate Calculation Worksheet – (cont'd)			
Step #5 From the marketing plan, determine: a. Existing Customers: The level of marketing expenditure required to support the sales team in selling to existing customers. (Include dedicated personnel costs, if necessary.)			
b. Self-Generation Sales Support: The level of marketing expenditure required to support the sales team to self-generate revenue			
c. New Customer Acquisition: The remaining marketing expenditure required to support revenue growth through acquisition of new customers			
Step #6 Calculate the base ROMI Hurdle Rate	**Base Hurdle Rates**	**Planning Contingency Factor (from Step #3)**	**Low Risk Hurdle Rates**
a. Existing Customers			
b. Self-Generation Sales Support			
c. New Customer Acquisition			
Step #7 Determine the ROMI Hurdle Rates by risk level	**Low Risk Hurdle Rates (from Step #6)**	**Medium Risk Hurdle Rates**	**High Risk Hurdle Rates**
a. Existing Customers			
b. Self-Generation Sales Support			
c. New Customer Acquisition			

Notes:

Step #1

Is the margin significantly different across the product line? (If yes, then you must use a margin based ROMI calculation. It not, you can simplify the work and use a revenue based ROMI calculation. A good rule of thumb is a difference greater than 5-10% for it to make sense to use a margin based calculation.)

Step #2

Are there specific types of personnel dedicated to marketing activities that need to be treated separately? Are there plans to add personnel throughout the year?

Step #3

What was your marketing program success rate from the prior year? How many marketing programs, percentage-wise, yielded significantly lower results than expected? The Planning Contingency Factor is 100% + (100%-failure rate).

Step #6

Divide revenue (margin) goal from Step #4 by planned marketing expenditures from Step #5. This rate is the base ROMI Hurdle Rate. Multiply by the Planning Contingency Factor and calculate the low risk ROMI Hurdle Rates.

Step #7

Determine ROMI Hurdle Rates for Mid and High Risk Marketing Plans by using a weighting. A good rule of thumb would be to use +33% for Medium Risk and +67% for High Risk Hurdle Rates.over the Low Risk Hurdle Rate. For example, if the Low Risk Hurdle Rate were 3.0, the Medium Risk Hurdle Rate would be 4.0 and the High Risk Hurdle Rate would be 5.0.

Sample ROMI Calculation Worksheet – Direct Mail

This worksheet provides a sample ROMI calculation worksheet for a combined direct mail program and compares it to the ROMI Hurdle Rate.

Sample ROMI Calculation Worksheet – Direct Mail		
	Example	**Your Program**
Program Description	Combined direct mail and telemarketing to 1,000 prospective companies in banking segment, 3 drops, includes direct mail piece creative and 3 dial attempts	
Step #1 Determine ROMI type, revenue or margin based	Revenue	
Step #2 Determine estimated program cost	$18,000	
Step #3 Determine estimated program return: a. Lead generation	Hot: 2% Warm: 5% Cold: 3%	
b. Determine expected revenue (margin) per sale	$5,000	
c. Determine close rates	Hot: 33% < 3mo. Warm: 20% 3-6 mo. Cold: 10% > 6mo.	
d. Determine estimated program revenue	Hot: $33,000 Warm: $50,000 Cold: $15,000 Total: $98,000	
Step #4 Determine program risk level	Low	
Step #5 Determine program ROMI	5.4	
Step #6 Compare with ROMI Hurdle Rate for program risk level	4.5	

Notes:

    Step #2

    In determining the estimated program cost be sure to include all incremental costs including personnel.

    Step #3

        a. Calculation methodologies may differ. In this example, leads were broken down into Hot,

Warm and Cold categories, each with some probability of closing over time.

b. In this case a simple estimation of the revenue per sale was used. If this differs widely, an average closing value should be used. If you are using margin based ROMI, enter estimated program margin here.

c. Not all leads will close. Use historical closing rates to estimate the potential closing rates the sales team may have.

d. Calculate total estimated program revenue (margin).

Step #4

Based on your estimate of the risks and uncertainties assign a risk level to the program. Typically, direct marketing activities with good prior experience can be considered low risk. If this is a direct mail program to a new market segment or there are other risks and uncertainties, use a higher risk level. Brand awareness oriented programs are typically assigned a higher risk level.

Step #5

Calculate the program ROMI by dividing the expected total program revenue (margin) from Step #3d by the estimated program cost from Step #2.

Step #6

Compare program ROMI with required ROMI Hurdle Rate. If expected program ROMI is not high enough go back to the program assumptions and determine if there are ways to increase the revenue (margin) or reduce program cost.

Suggestions:

- Simply changing the estimated program returns from Step #3a or the estimated closing rates from Step #3d is not recommended.
- Look for ways to increase the expected revenue per sale from Step #3b.

- Look for ways to reduce the estimated program cost from Step #2.

For additional worksheets, please send your request to romi@returnonmarketing.*net*.

Tables and Figures

Tables

Figures

Index

Index of Examples

Bibliography

Books

Baker, Wayne E. *Networking Smart: How to Build Relationships for Personal and Organizational Success.* New York: McGraw-Hill, Inc., 1994.

Coleman, Chris. *The Green Banana Papers: Marketing Secrets for Technology Entrepreneurs.* Atlanta: St. Barthelemy Press, 2001.

Covey, Stephen R. *The Seven Habits of Highly Effective People.* New York: Simon & Schuster, 1990.

Gates, Bill. *Business @ the Speed of Thought.* New York: Warner Books, 1999.

Kieran, T.K., *Tactics for Measuring ROMI (Return on Marketing Investment),* Atlanta: Presentation to Business Marketing Association, April, 2002.

Mackay, Harvey. *Swim With the Sharks (Without Being Eaten Alive).* New York: Fawcett Book Group, 1996.

Maxwell, John C. *The 21 Irrefutable Laws of Leadership.* Nashville: Thomas Nelson, 1998.

Moore, Geoffrey A. *Crossing the Chasm.* New York: Harper Business, 1995.

Moore, Geoffrey A. *Inside the Tornado.* New York: Harper Business, 1995.

Page, Rick. *Hope Is Not A Strategy.* Atlanta: Nautilus Press, 2002.

Peters, Thomas J. and Robert H. Waterman, Jr. *In Search of Excellence.* New York: Warner Books, 1988.

Porter, Michael E. *Competitive Advantage.* New York: Simon & Schuster, 1998.

Porter, Michael E. *Competitive Strategy*. New York: Simon & Schuster, 1998.

Ries, Al and Jack Trout. *Marketing Warfare*. New York: McGraw-Hill, 1997.

Ries, Al and Jack Trout. *Positioning: The Battle for Your Mind*. New York: Warner Books, 1986.

Ries, Al and Laura Ries. *The Fall of Advertising, the Rise of PR*. New York: Cahners Business Information, Inc., 2002.

Ziglar, Zig. *Ziglar on Selling*. Ballantine Books, 1991.

Websites and Newsletters

Accenture Ideas, www.accenture.com.

bitpipe, www.bitpipe.com.

ClickZ Marketing, www.clickz.com.

INSIDER PASS Newsletter, www.technologymarketing.com.

MarketingSherpaWeekly, www.marketingsherpa.com.

MarketingProgs, www.marketingprofs.com.

Software Success, www.softwaresuccess.com.

Technology Marketing, www.technologymarketing.com.

The Direct Marketing Association, www.the-dma.org.

KnowThis.com, www.knowthis.com.

The American Marketing Association, www.ama.org

The New York American Marketing Association, www.nyama.org.